Anzio: bid for Rome

Anzio: bid for Rome

Editor-in-Chief: Barrie Pitt
Art Director: Peter Dunbar

Military Consultant: Sir Basil Liddell Hart
Picture Editor: Bobby Hunt

Editor: David Mason
Design: Sarah Kingham
Cover: Denis Piper
Cartographer: Richard Natkiel
Special Drawings : John Batchelor

Photographs for this book were especially selected from the following archives.
From left to right page 2–3 US Army; 9 Imperial War Museum; 10 US Army; 14–15 US Air Force; 18 Sado Opera Mundi;
19 Sado Opera Mundi/Ullstein; 20–22 IWM; 24–27 US Army; 29 Bundesarchiv; 31 US Army; 32–33 US Navy; 34 IWM/US Army;
35 US Army; 36–39 IWM; 40–41 US Army; 42–46 IWM; 50 Bundesarchiv; 51 US Army; 52 IWM; 53 IWM/US Army; 54–55 US
Air Force; 56–59 IWM; 60–61 Ullstein/US Navy/US Navy; 62–65 IWM; 68–69 US Army; 73 Ullstein; 74 IWM; 75–79 US Army;
80–81 IWM; 82–83 Bundesarchiv; 84–85 IWM; 86 Heinrich Hoffmann; 88–89 Bundesarchiv; 93 Ullstein; 94–95 Sado Opera Mundi;
96–97 Bundesarchiv; 97 Bibliothek für Zeitgeschichte; 99 Ullstein; 100–103 US Army; 104–105 US Air Force; 106 US Army; 107 IWM;
112–114 Sado Opera Mundi; 114–115 US Army; 117 Heinrich Hoffmann; 118 US Army/IWM; 122–123 IWM; 124–125 US Navy;
130 IWM; 132–135 US Army; 136–140 The Psywar Society; 142–143 IWM; 144–145 Bundesarchiv; 148 Heinrich Hoffmann;
149 Sado Opera Mundi; 150 US Army; 151 US Army/IWM; 152–153 IWM; 154–155 US Army

First published in the United States of America.
This edition first published in Great Britain
in 1970 by Macdonald & Co. (Publishers) Ltd
49 Poland Street, London W1.

Printed in Great Britain by
Hazell Watson & Viney Ltd, Aylesbury, Bucks

Contents

Another Gallipoli?

Introduction by Barrie Pitt

It is hard to avoid seeing in Operation Shingle, the landing at Anzio, features which recall the First World War landing at Gallipoli, as the Corps Commander General Lucas noted.

Like that operation, Shingle was one of Winston Churchill's obsessions, one of the 'cat's claw' manoeuvres for which he had such high hopes. Also like that operation, Shingle would have been immensely useful had it gone according to plan; had the outcome been totally successful, it would have brought to Churchill the praise for inspired thinking that success deserves and failure, by however short a margin, denies. Like that operation, the landing which should have led to a devastating thrust degenerated into a campaign of attrition, in which the static trench warfare called to mind other terrible battles of the First World War. But unlike the Gallipoli operation, the outcome was not a withdrawal, although the German defenders almost succeeded in inflicting that ignominy on the Allies, but an eventual break-through, leading to the capture of the first Axis capital of the war.

Churchill's obsession apart, what were the aims of the Anzio landing?

The decision to invade southern Italy in the autumn of 1943 stemmed from the conference held by Churchill, Roosevelt, and the Combined Chiefs of Staff at Casablanca in the preceding January. Once the Allies had secured the Mediterranean sea lanes by their conquests in North Africa and Sicily, they were in some disagreement about where to go next. The British and American commands agreed that the cross-Channel invasion into Normandy was to be the decisive thrust against the weakening enemy, but beyond that their views diverged. General Marshall, the US Army Chief of Staff, feared that a landing in Italy would absorb resources needed for the cross-Channel invasion. Churchill and the British, on the other hand, were keen to engage Hitler in a campaign in the Mediterranean, to draw off German resources from France and the Low Countries. Conquest of Italy would present the additional benefit of airfields to bomb the German war factories and Rumanian oilfields.

When it became obvious that no cross-Channel invasion could be staged during 1943, the prospects for a campaign beyond Sicily became feasible, and when the relatively easy invasion of Sicily and the downfall of Mussolini rendered the prospects even more inviting, Eisenhower, the Allied Commander-in-Chief, secured approval for a landing on the Italian mainland.

In fact there were three landings, all in early September, across the Straits of Messina by Montgomery's Eighth Army, in the Gulf of Taranto by the 1st Airborne Division of Eighth Army, and in the Gulf of Salerno near Naples by General Mark Clark's Fifth Army. The first two of these went virtually unopposed, but the Salerno operation met determined resistance from Field-Marshal Kesselring's Panzer Divisions, and almost ran into disaster. Eventually, on 1st October 1943, Clark's forces entered Naples, and drove on until they were finally stopped again on the River Volturno on 7th October.

From then until the end of the year the situation in Italy remained one of stalemate, and the landing at Anzio came into prominence as a means of breaking the deadlock. It was intended as one half of a decisive pincer movement on western Italy. The bulk of the American Fifth Army would attack northwards in a land operation against the German defensive line, the Gustav Line, while the VI Corps landed behind the Gustav line. Whichever way the Germans moved would leave the way open for Allied victory: if they defended against the frontal assault, the troops landed in Operation Shingle would be able to penetrate their lines of communication; if they counterattacked against the landing their Gustav Line defenses would be weakened. That, in broad outline, was the theory. But inevitably subsequent developments perversely refused to conform. Firstly there was a further brilliantly organised and superbly fought defensive action by the Germans, led again by Kesselring and General Vietinghoff, which threatened to succeed where the defence at Salerno had failed and cut the beachhead in half with a counterattack. Then there was the pathetic indecisiveness of the VI Corps commander General Lucas who, abetted by General Clark, refused to seize the opportunity presented at the beginning of the invasion, and concentrated on building up his resources, while the Germans at the same time concentrated on deploying their defences. And finally there was the highly dubious action of Clark himself, who set his heart on a triumphant entry into Rome rather than on defeating the enemy.

In this book Christopher Hibbert examines all these aspects of the Anzio operation, and gives an enthralling account of the bitter fighting, backing his customary meticulous research with intelligent analysis.

Overall, the picture that emerges is one of lack of faith among the Allied leaders. Whether the Anzio operation fulfilled any purpose at all, by for example keeping German divisions away from the front in Normandy, is open to question. As Christopher Hibbert points out, probably the most useful outcome lay in the lessons its failure provided for the cross-Channel invasion itself. If that is all it did, it cannot be accounted other than an expensive failure. But then, one tends to judge everything, unjustly perhaps, by the highest standard, contrasting the Anzio operation with that in Normandy. What other story might now be told if the Allies had enjoyed the same quality of leadership in western Italy that they enjoyed in northern France, combining the singlemindedness of Marshall, the administrative skill of Eisenhower, the intelligence of Bradley, and decisiveness of Patton, and the nerve of Montgomery? But Anzio never carried the once-and-for-all finality of the Normandy landings. Nobody, not even Churchill, cared about it quite as much, and the entire half-hearted operation fell short of being a great amphibious landing.

In those circumstances, perhaps it is hardly surprising that Churchill could lament: 'I had hoped that we would be hurling a wildcat ashore, but all we got was a stranded whale.'

Stalemate in Italy

'We are in full agreement with you that the present stagnation cannot be allowed to continue.' – the British Chiefs of Staff to the Prime Minister, 22nd December 1943.

In December 1943 General Sir Alan Brooke, Chief of the Imperial General Staff, made a tour of the Italian front. He was very disheartened by what he saw and heard. After a visit to the headquarters of General Sir Bernard Montgomery's British Eighth Army on the Sangro River, he noted in his diary, 'Monty strikes me as looking tired and definitely wants a rest and change. I can see that he does not feel that [General Mark] Clark is running the [American] Fifth Army right, nor that Alex [General the Hon. Sir Harold Alexander, Commander-in-Chief of the Allied Armies in Italy] is gripping the show sufficiently... Monty called me into his caravan just before dinner and asked me how much importance we attached to an early capture of Rome, as he saw little hope of capturing it before March. To my mind it is quite

clear there is no real plan for the capture of Rome... Frankly I am rather depressed.'

The next day Brooke's depression deepened. It was becoming ever more obvious to him that the offensive in Italy was 'stagnating badly', that the commanders had lost their spirit and drive. Not only was Montgomery stale and tired, but Alexander had evidently not yet recovered from the debilitating effects of a recent attack of jaundice. Mark Clark, with whom Brooke dined on 16th December, did nothing to reassure him. After a long talk with the Fifth Army commander, Brooke did not feel 'very cheered up as to the prospects of the future'. Clark seemed to be 'planning nothing but penny-packet attacks'. Something, Brooke decided, must be done immediately.

The Fifth Army had landed in the Gulf of Salerno, south of Naples, on 9th December 1943. The Germans had fought a delaying action in Sicily, and although they had lost 37,000 men during the campaign, against Allied losses of just over 31,000, they had

managed to evacuate 60,000 men and a considerable amount of equipment to the mainland. So they were able to bring the weight of five full divisions immediately into action at Salerno, and they had almost succeeded in compelling the Americans to re-embark. It was not until 15th September, indeed, that the overwhelming superiority of Allied air support had ensured the safety of the beachhead and the immediate danger was past. On 16th December, the British Eighth Army, which had landed unopposed at Reggio on the 3rd and had subsequently advanced two hundred miles, made contact with the Americans about forty miles southeast of Salerno.

The Allies now advanced north by different routes, the Americans on the west coast through Naples, which fell on 1st October, the British on the east coast by way of Bari, Foggia and Termoli. By the time of Brooke's visit, however, the Allied offensive had ground to a standstill on the rivers that now blocked their path, the Garigliano and the Sangro. Behind these

Generals Alexander, Montgomery, and Brooke on a visit to Montgomery's Eighth Army Front

rivers the Germans rapidly improved the defences of the Gustav Line that stretched across Italy from the Mediterranean to the Adriatic, from the Aurunci mountains to Ortona. The road from Naples to Rome passed through this line beneath a mountain whose name was to become cruelly familiar to the Allied soldiers—Monte Cassino. As Hitler advised his Commander-in-Chief in Italy, the Gustav Line was to 'mark the end of withdrawals'.

A situation had now developed in Italy which the Chiefs of Staff in Washington had been anxious to avoid. For at the Casablanca Conference held at the beginning of the year, it had been agreed that there would be a cross-Channel invasion of France in the early summer of 1944. And in the American view, this invasion, to be given code-name Operation Overlord, must be given overriding priority: everything else must be subordinated to it. The worse

thing that could happen, they considered, would be to get heavily committed to an expensive and exhausting campaign in southern Europe which would drain Operation Overlord of the dynamic strength that alone would ensure its success. Deeply concerned about the war in the Pacific, they wanted – as also the Russians wanted – a quick, strong blow against the Axis, a decisive thrust by the shortest route to Berlin.

The British, on the other hand, with their eyes on Malta, Gibraltar, Egypt and the oil fields of the Middle East, had good and traditional reasons for being vitally anxious to keep control of the Mediterranean. They maintained that pressure on the Russian front, combined with pressure in the Mediterranean, could not but weaken Germany and render her less likely, when the moment came, to be able to hold back the Allies in Normandy.

The British further argued that a campaign in Italy would help Overlord rather than weaken it. For it would serve to pin down, south of the Alps, German divisions which would otherwise be available to fight in Germany. All very well, the Americans countered, but what if it were the enemy who were pinning down valuable Allied divisions in Italy and holding them there, in country that might have been made for defence, at no great expense to themselves? Certainly the British High Command underestimated, to a more serious extent than the American Command, the problems of offensive warfare in the Italian peninsula. An advance northwards along either coastline was rendered peculiarly difficult because of the succession of rivers that ran across the narrow coastal plains; an advance up the middle of the country was out of the question owing to the rugged mountain ranges. Superiority in armoured units

Lieutenant-General Clark, Fifth Army commander, looks thoughtful as he goes ashore on the first day of Operation Shingle

was unavailing in country such as this; superiority in air power was valueless in the appalling winter weather soon to come.

As one American officer put it, Italy would be a far tougher nut to crack than blithe talk about the 'soft underbelly of Europe' seemed to imply. It would be far better, in American opinion, to go for Sardinia and Corsica as stepping-stones to the south of France. Yet the opportunities offered by a successful campaign in Italy, so persuasively argued by the British, had been tempting enough to overcome the active opposition of all but the most sceptical. For to capture Naples and Rome would be undoubtedly crippling blows to the Axis; they might well lead to the surrender of Italy and the withdrawal of German forces to the north; they would certainly lead to the Allies coming into possession of valuable airfields and a base from which the Balkans and the south of France might be threatened. The opportunities presented by the Italian campaign seemed somewhat more remote now that the Allied offensive had been so firmly halted in the cold and muddy river valleys beneath the formidable defences of the Gustav Line. But they had not yet been missed. Once the crust of opposition had been broken and the Germans forced into retreat again, the Italian campaign might yet offer the rewards that its most sanguine advocates had predicted.

To achieve these rewards, however, strong and immediate action, as Brooke had decided, was vital. The temporary stalemate on the Italian front must on no account be allowed to degenerate into a permanent one. If the Gustav Line was already so strong that a frontal assault was not at the moment practicable, why not outflank it by a seaborne invasion? This idea had already been mooted in Italy before Brooke's arrival when it had been planned to land a division supported by paratroops on the coast about thirty miles south of Rome. After Brooke's departure for England he strongly urged that it be discussed again. The

11

scheme had another, even more powerful advocate.

On 17th December, while Brooke was still in Italy, the Prime Minister sent a message to President Roosevelt. 'Am stranded amid the ruins of Carthage with fever which has ripened into pneumonia,' Churchill dictated. 'All your people are doing everything possible, but I do not pretend I am enjoying myself. I hope soon to send you some of the suggestions for the new commands...'

Although constantly advised to rest, persistently enjoined by his doctors, 'Don't work, don't worry', Churchill could not relax. His mind was preoccupied with the problems of war, and although he allowed his daughter, Sarah, to read him *Pride and Prejudice* to take his mind off the excitements and burdens of office, he could not remain still or unoccupied for long. His thoughts kept returning to the numerous important matters raised and discussed at the recent tiring conferences at Teheran and Cairo. One of the questions uppermost in his mind, as he had implied in his message to Roosevelt, was the selection of officers for the various important commands in Operation Overlord. He dealt with this problem in a telegram to Roosevelt dated 18th December.

It had already been decided that General Eisenhower, until then Commander-in-Chief of the Allied Expeditionary Forces in the Mediterranean should be recalled to the Supreme Command of the Allied Expeditionary Force in Western Europe. The British General Sir Henry Maitland Wilson was chosen to succeed him with the American General Jacob L Devers as Deputy Commander.

General Alexander, as Commander-in-Chief of the Armies in Italy, was left in control of the 15th Army Group, comprising the British Eighth and the American Fifth Armies. Mark Clark retained command of the Fifth Army; Lieutenant-General Sir Oliver Leese took over the Eighth Army from Montgomery who was appointed to command the cross-Channel invasion force. When these and other appointments had been settled, Churchill turned his attention to the Italian campaign which had always been very close to his heart. He had, as he had often made clear, a 'very strong desire' to capture Rome. 'Nothing less than Rome,' he insisted, 'could satisfy the requirements of this year's campaign.'

General Brooke had declined to discuss Italy in detail with him when he came to say goodbye to him on 18th December. Churchill was in 'very good form', Brooke thought. His wife who had flown out from England to join him was sitting on his bed; his son, Randolph, was there too. Brooke was careful not to cast a shadow across the Prime Minister's cheerful mood by mentioning the 'depressing impression' he had gained from his recent travels. Also, 'I knew from experience,' he wrote later, 'that he would only want to rush into some solution which would probably make matters worse ... Winston's lack of "width" and "depth" in the examination of problems was a factor I never got over. He would select an individual piece of the vast jigsaw puzzle which we had in front of us and concentrate on it at the expense of all others.'

In the solution to the problem of the Italian *impasse*, however, Brooke did not quarrel with Churchill's enthusiasm for a landing behind the Gustav Line in conjunction with an attack by the main armies. Churchill had always favoured this sort of manoeuvre which made a natural appeal to his temperament. He called it a 'cat's claw' in contrast to the American term, 'end run'; and he had long regretted that he had been unable to persuade the generals to make use of it in any of the desert advances. Now was his opportunity to put it into operation, to employ the Allies' sea-power in an exciting venture that could bring great rewards.

As well as to Brooke, the idea appealed to Alexander and to Eisenhower. And General Wilson, who was to suc-

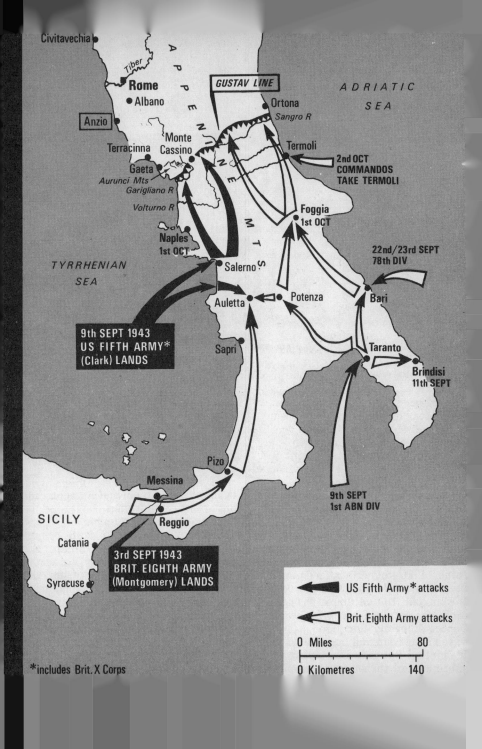

Civitavechia

Tiber

APPENNINE

Rome
● Albano

GUSTAV LINE

Anzio

Terracinna
Monte
Cassino
Gaeta
Aurunci Mts
Garigliano R
Volturno R

ADRIATIC
SEA

● Ortona
Sangro R

Termoli ← 2nd OCT
COMMANDOS
TAKE TERMOLI

Foggia
1st OCT

22nd/23rd SEPT
78th DIV

TYRRHENIAN
SEA

Naples
1st OCT

Salerno

Auletta ← Potenza

Bari

9th SEPT 1943
US FIFTH ARMY*
(Clark) LANDS

Sapri

Taranto → Brindisi
11th SEPT

Pizo

9th SEPT
1st ABN DIV

Messina

SICILY

Reggio

Catania

3rd SEPT 1943
BRIT. EIGHTH ARMY
(Montgomery) LANDS

Syracuse

◀ US Fifth Army* attacks

◁ Brit. Eighth Army attacks

0   Miles   80

0   Kilometres   140

*includes Brit. X Corps

Littorio airfield, Rome, eliminated as a factor in the Italian campaign by Allied bombers

ceed Eisenhower agreed that it was a good idea to make a flanking attack rather than to get 'bogged down in the mountains'. Even General George C Marshall, United States Army Chief of Staff, on whose advice President Roosevelt firmly depended, approved of the plan. Marshall had always made it clear that in his opinion the operations in the Mediterranean must never be allowed to assume so great an importance that the success of Operation Overlord was placed in jeopardy, and that the time might come when the Italian campaign would have to be discontinued altogether; but now he agreed that Rome and its important aerodromes ought to be taken as quickly as possible.

Eisenhower's Chief of Staff, Major-General Walter Bedell Smith, Air Chief-Marshal Sir Arthur Tedder of the Mediterranean Air Command, and Admiral Sir Andrew Cunningham of the Naval Command also supported the venture; and although all these officers were soon to leave the Mediterranean for appointments in Western Europe, their successors were equally satisfied that the plan was a sound one. But none of them could match the Prime Minister's excited enthusiasm. He dismissed the objections of Brigadier KWD Strong, chief Intelligence officer at Eisenhower's headquarters, who thought that the

head until the Allies were too strong to be thrown back.

On the day after Brooke left for England, Churchill sent an urgent and angrily worded telegram to the Chiefs of Staff: 'I am anxiously awaiting a full list of all landing-craft of all types in the Mediterranean now, showing their condition and employment, and especially whether it is true that a large number are absorbed in purely supply work to the prevention of their amphibious duties. There is no doubt that the stagnation of the whole campaign on the Italian front is becoming scandalous. [Brooke's] . . . visit confirmed my worst forebodings. The total neglect to provide amphibious action on the Adriatic and the failure to strike any similar blow on the west have been disastrous. None of the landing-craft in the Mediterranean have been put to the slightest use for three months. . . . There are few instances, even in this war, of such valuable forces being so completely wasted.

In their reply the Chiefs of Staff expressed their 'full agreement' that the present stagnation could not be allowed to continue. For every reason it was essential that something should be done to speed things up. 'The solution as you say,' they continued, 'clearly lies in making use of our amphibious power to strike round on the enemy's flank and open up the way for a rapid advance on Rome.'

Before any detailed plans for an amphibious operation could be made, however, far more specialised landing-craft than were at present available in Italy would have to be collected. The most vital of these craft were DUKWS (amphibious motor-lorries), LCAs (Landing Craft, Assault), LCIs (Landing Craft, Infantry), LCTs (Landing Craft, Tanks), LSIs (Landing Ships, Infantry) and LSTs (Landing Ships, Tanks). The last of these, the LSTs, the biggest of them all, were absolutely indispensable. And they, difficult enough to assemble in sufficient quantities in the Mediterranean at the best of times, would be in even more acutely

Germans were too strong in Italy for a landing behind the Gustav Line to be successful. He allowed Strong to voice his opinion, but only after the decision to make the landing had been arrived at, and then with the dismissive remark, 'Well, we may as well hear the seamy side of the question'.

Mark Clark's Intelligence staff shared Strong's apprehensions, warning that the landing would be 'met by all the resources and strength available to the German High Command in Italy.' Churchill set more store by Alexander's Intelligence officers who were more hopeful, suggesting that the Germans had no more than two divisions in reserve near Rome and that the Allied air forces would be able to prevent reinforcements arriving at the beach-

15

The Landing Craft Infantry (Large) was one of the earliest US landing craft, and featured side ramps instead of the later bow landing doors. It weighed 246 tons and was armed with five 20mm cannon. Powered by 2-shaft diesel motors delivering 2,320 brake horse power, it was capable of 14.4 knots. Its dimensions were 159 feet by $23\frac{3}{4}$ feet by $5\frac{3}{4}$ feet and had a crew of 25

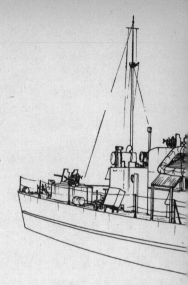

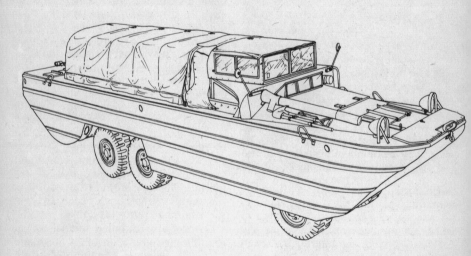

The Landing Craft Tank (4) was an adaptation of the basic tank landing craft design, which had a crew of twelve and a capacity of twelve 40-ton tanks or ten 3-ton trucks. It was capable of 10.5 knots and was armed with two 2-pounders or two 20mm Oerlikon cannon

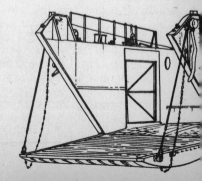

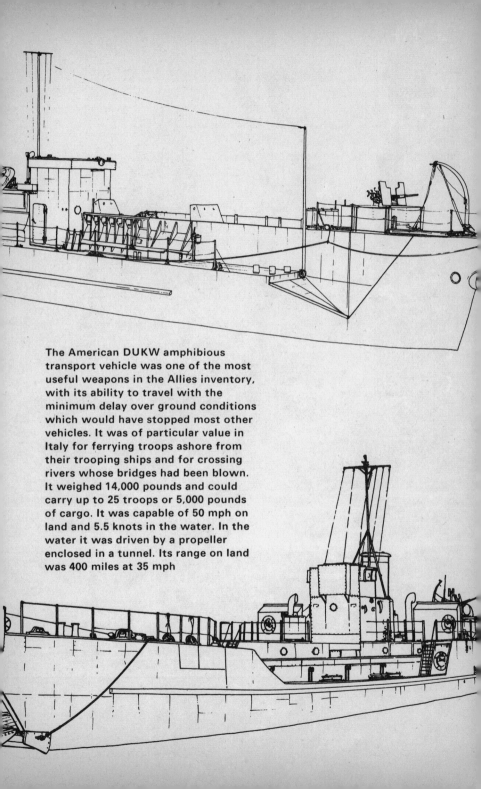

The American DUKW amphibious
transport vehicle was one of the most
useful weapons in the Allies inventory,
with its ability to travel with the
minimum delay over ground conditions
which would have stopped most other
vehicles. It was of particular value in
Italy for ferrying troops ashore from
their trooping ships and for crossing
rivers whose bridges had been blown.
It weighed 14,000 pounds and could
carry up to 25 troops or 5,000 pounds
of cargo. It was capable of 50 mph on
land and 5.5 knots in the water. In the
water it was driven by a propeller
enclosed in a tunnel. Its range on land
was 400 miles at 35 mph

The German defenders wait for the invasion that will follow the Allies' conquest of Sicily

short supply after 15th January when most of those already in the area would be withdrawn for Operation Overlord. There would then be enough for little more than one division to be put ashore north of the Gustav Line; and a landing limited to one division would be more than likely to end in disaster unless the Fifth Army were much closer in support than it was at present. Ideally the operation which Churchill had in mind would entail the use of three divisions; but to collect sufficient LSTs for such a large force was out of the question. If strict economies were made elsewhere in the Mediterranean, however, if additional craft could be supplied from other theatres of war, and if LSTs on their way back to England for the Normandy invasion were delayed for a time, it might be possible to mount an attack with two divisions. But this would necessitate certain other projects being abandoned, as well as a delay in the date of Operation Overlord.

Would Washington agree to this? Churchill himself was resigned to abandoning an amphibious operation which had been planned to take place on the Arakan coast of Burma, and, more reluctantly, to give up the idea of capturing Rhodes. But the British Chiefs of Staff very much doubted that the Americans would agree to a delay in Operation Overlord. Indeed, when Churchill asked Bedell Smith to suggest that the LSTs due to leave for Overlord should be kept in the Mediterranean until 15th February, Bedell Smith replied that he dared not even propose such a thing. Clearly Churchill would need all his powers of persuasion to gain the Americans' consent.

There were, he was told, 104 LSTs in the Mediterranean at the moment; but if all those due to take part in Overlord left as planned on 15th February, there would be only thirty-six left. Fifteen others were due to arrive from the Indian Ocean, but these would not come in time to be used in Italy. To land two divisions, eighty-eight were required in all. Therefore, as Churchill wrote to the Chiefs of Staff

Above: The invasion fleet assembles in North Africa. *Right:* The first prisoners taken by the invasion forces

on Christmas Day, all the fifty-six LSTs due to depart from the Mediterranean for Overlord would have to be delayed 'for not more than a month'. On the same day he sent a telegram to President Roosevelt, putting forward his case. A landing by two divisions, he suggested, 'should decide the Battle of Rome, and possibly achieve the destruction of a substantial part of the enemy's army. To strike with less than two divisions would be to court disaster, having regard to the positions likely to be achieved by that date by the Fifth and Eighth Armies.

'For this purpose eighty-eight LSTs are required. These can only be obtained by delaying the return home of fifty-six LSTs due to leave the Mediterranean from January 15th onward... Nothing less than this will suffice. The fifteen LSTs from India cannot arrive in time...

'Having kept these fifty-six LSTs in

the Mediterranean so long, it would seem irrational to remove them for the very week when they can render decisive service. What, also, could be more dangerous than to let the Italian battle stagnate and fester on for another three months? We cannot afford to go forward leaving a vast half-finished job behind us... If this opportunity is not grasped we must expect the ruin of the Mediterranean campaign of 1944. I earnestly hope therefore that you may agree to the three weeks' delay in return of the fifty-six landing-craft . . .'.

Soon after this telegram was despatched, Churchill left Carthage for his 'beloved Marrakesh' where it was

The people of Italy learn the horrors of conflict in their land

hoped he could convalesce in peace and would put aside the problems of the Italian campaign until he had regained his strength. But in Marrakesh, as he admitted, one thing rose above all others in his mind – what answer would the President give to his telegram? When he thought of 'the dull, dead-weight resistance, taking no account of timing and proportion', that he had encountered, 'about all Mediterranean projects', he awaited the answer with deep anxiety. What he had asked for was a hazardous enterprise on the Italian coast, and a possible delay of three to four weeks in the date of the Channel crossing.

So it was with joy, as he confessed, 'not unmingled with surprise', that on 28th December he received this telegram from President Roosevelt: 'It

is agreed to delay the departure of fifty-six LSTs scheduled for Overlord... on the basis that Overlord remains the paramount operation...'. Churchill replied on the same day in a telegram expressive of his fervour: 'I thank God for this fine decision which engages us once again in wholehearted unity upon a great enterprise. I have heard from the British Chiefs of Staff that the Admiralty can conform to the conditions... the Chiefs of Staff will be telegraphing today in full detail to the Combined Chiefs of Staff. Meanwhile here the word is full steam ahead...'

Churchill thought that the President's telegram was 'a marvel'. He was sure that he owed it not only to Roosevelt's own personal goodwill but to the 'balance of mind' of General Marshall, to Eisenhower's 'loyalty to the show he was about to quit', and to Bedell Smith's 'active, knowledgeable, fact-armed diplomacy'. Indeed, nothing could have pleased the Prime Minister more than this submission by the Americans to his advice, this display of their trust in his judgement. When General Alexander sent to Marrakesh his plans for the forthcoming operation, Churchill was in an extremely contented frame of mind.

General Alexander's plan, formulated after a conference with General Clark, the American Fifth Army Commander, and General Brian Robertson, the Chief Administrative Officer at 15th Army Group Headquarters, was for a landing on the beaches around Anzio, a small port about thirty miles south of Rome.

Before the war Anzio had been a quiet seaside place, a pleasant two hours' drive from the capital. The town itself, its port and harbour, were built on a small promontory on either side of which were sandy beaches. Behind the beaches there were holiday villas in the pine woods.

A mile further away from Rome down the coast was another smaller town, Nettuno, an old town beneath whose narrow, medieval streets were a warren of catacombs and tunnels used as cellars for the maturing local wine. Southwards from Nettuno the coastline stretched towards Terracina, Gaeta and Naples, and inland, between the white beaches and the range of hills known as the Colli Lepini, there were the Pontine Marshes, drained at great expense by the Fascist Government, traversed by new canals, and dotted with the white farm settlements, where, in happier days, Il Duce, naked to the waist, loved to be photographed haranguing grateful workers, inheritors of the benefits of the Fascist State.

Beyond Anzio to the north, to a height of three thousand feet, there rise the Monti Albani, the Alban Hills, guarding the way to Rome. Around the foot of these hills curved the railroads and the highways that led from Naples to Rome. The more westerly of the two highways, Route 7, passed through Capua, across the Garigliano River close to its mouth, then up through Cisterna and Velletri, curving round south of the Alban Hills, then into Rome. The other highway, Route 6, which passed the Alban Hills to the North, went through Mignano, Cassino and Valmontone.

It was clear from the briefest glance at the map that a landing at Anzio, followed by a push towards the Alban Hills and through Velletri, in the valley between the hills and the Colli Lepini, would not only threaten Rome but would also endanger the lines of communication of the Germans fighting on the Gustav Line.

It was decided to land two divisions on the beaches either side of Anzio, one British division, one American. The two divisions, supported by paratroops and commandos, would be placed under an American corps commander. Ten days before the landing, there would be a powerful offensive against the Gustav Line in the area of Cassino which, it was hoped, would draw off most of the German reserves south of Rome. The landing was scheduled for about 20th January; the operation was to be given the code-name Shingle. This was the bare outline of the plan;

but as soon as the detailed work on it began, numerous difficulties presented themselves. The first difficulty was that there seemed to be no parachute troops available for the operation. The British Parachute Brigade was fighting in the line, and there was no unit with which Alexander could relieve them. The 504th American Parachute Regiment was due to leave the theatre, and Eisenhower was reluctant to press for its retention.

As soon as he learned of the problem, Churchill leaped into action again. He cabled Field Marshal Sir John Dill, the representative of the British Chiefs of Staff in Washington, and asked him to appeal to General Marshall and to Eisenhower, who was now with him, if they would 'let this 504th American Regiment do this one fine and critical job before they come home for "Overlord". It is so rarely,' Churchill's plea continued, 'that opportunities for decisive air action by paratroops present themselves, and it seems improvident to take them from the decisive point just when they might render exemplary and outstanding service. They can be sent home immediately afterwards in time for "Overlord"...'

On this issue, as over the retention of the LSTs, the Americans deferred to the British Prime Minister's wishes. But then there were further problems when it was discovered that the agreement to return the LSTs to England for the Normandy invasion after the landing at Anzio would mean that the two divisions could not be adequately supplied and maintained. General Alexander explained the dilemma to Churchill: 'The removal of all but six of the LSTs after the initial landing will not allow us to put the two divisions ashore complete with their essential fighting vehicles... My experience of combined operations is that the initial assault to get ashore can be effected, but the success of the operation depends on whether the full fighting strength of the expedition can be concentrated in time

to withstand the inevitable counter-attack... We are willing to accept any risks to achieve our object, but if the two divisions get sealed off by the Germans we obviously cannot leave them there without any support... Clark and I are confident that we have a great chance of pulling off something big if given the means with which to do it'.

The means, Alexander insisted, included fourteen LSTs to be left in the Mediterranean until the troops landed at Anzio had linked up with the advancing Fifth Army, and a further ten LSTs for a period of fifteen days after the landing so as to build up the two divisions in guns, tanks and other supporting arms to a strength sufficient for them to fight on equal terms with the Germans. Even if this interfered with the projected landing in the South of France, surely the prize was worth it?

Churchill, who had no doubt as to what the right answer to that question should be, once again called in all the authorities concerned and then went into lively action on behalf of the Anzio operation. On this occasion, too, he was successful. The President concurred.

By his energetic efforts at Carthage and Marrakesh – although he was still so weak and exhausted that he could

Salerno, where Clark 'stuck his neck out'

24

not face painting, could hardly walk, and spent eighteen hours a day in bed – Churchill eventually managed to get as many as eighty-eight LSTs for Operation Shingle which had now become recognised amongst his associates as one of those schemes so dear to his heart that nothing must be allowed to stand in the way of their success. Not that Operation Shingle, at this stage in its planning, was one of those schemes, so dreaded in London, which would have been immediately dropped had it not had so powerful and single-minded an advocate. It had many other supporters in addition to Churchill.

Intelligence reports now gave these supporters every encouragement. At 15th Army Group Headquarters it was held that Operation Shingle would lead to the enemy being manoeuvred out of his positions around Cassino. At Fifth Army Headquarters, where reports of a sharp decline in German morale were happily circulating, it was believed that the enemy's strength on the Cassino front was weakening, that it was doubtful that he could hold the Gustav Line against a co-ordinated enemy attack. 'Since this attack is to be launched before Shingle,' one Intelligence report advised, 'it is considered likely that this additional threat will cause him to withdraw from his defensive position once he has appreciated the magnitude of that operation.'

The Air Forces staffs were quite as optimistic as Intelligence. Allied aircraft in Italy outnumbered German by almost six to one, and with this immense superiority in air power it seemed impossible to suppose that the beachhead could not be isolated, that the enemy's communications and supply lines could not be devastated.

In the event the Germans were to show not only how well they had adapted themselves to the loss of that air cover they had enjoyed during the earlier part of the war, but how well they managed both to fight and to move troops and supplies despite the fact that control of the skies had passed into the hands of the British and American Air Forces. They had become adept at moving by night and at taking every advantage of periods of bad weather when flying was impossible. But at the time it seemed that with command of the air and of the seas, the land forces – even though there were only two divisions of them – were embarking upon Operation Shingle with exceptional advantages.

Anzio and Nettuno, the site chosen for the landing

Operation Shingle

'I felt like a lamb being led to the slaughter... I have the bare minimum of ships and craft . . . The force that can be gotten ashore in a hurry is weak and I haven't sufficient artillery to hold me over.' Major-General John P Lucas, VI Corps Commander: diary entry for 9th January 1944.

The two divisions selected to take part in Operation Shingle were the American 3rd Infantry Division, and the British 1st Infantry Division. The 3rd Division had landed at Licata in Sicily and had been given the task of capturing the town and airfield. As part of General George S Patton's II Corps, it had distinguished itself in the ensuing campaign. It had been landed at Salerno on 18th September and had made a successful night attack on Avellino on the 19th. Subsequently it had played a leading part in the crossing of the Volturno. The Division had been brought out of the line when the idea of a landing near Rome was first mooted, and had been concentrated near Naples.

Its commander was General Lucian K Truscott, Jr, a forthright, grey-haired, forty-nine-year-old officer with a confident, assertive, if somewhat taciturn manner and a distinguished record. Invariably he wore a leather battle jacket, a steel helmet and tall boots; he looked, and was, tough. His troops knew him, with some affection and more esteem, as 'Old Gravel Mouth'. He had been sent to London when America declared war and had grown to appreciate the virtues of the British who, in turn, liked him.

The British Division, the 1st Infantry Division, had proved its worth in Tunisia. It had since captured the small island of Pantelleria between Sicily and the Tunisian coast, and had thereafter been held in reserve, first in North Africa and then near Foggia.

Its commander was Major-General W R C Penney. Like Truscott, Penney was very much a front-line general. He

Field-Marshal Kesselring, Commander-in-Chief in Italy

was slightly younger than his American colleague; but he had had an extremely varied and active career, having been commissioned into the Royal Engineers at the beginning of the First World War and having served on the North West Frontier of India in the 1930s. He had been awarded the DSO as well as the MC, the French as well as the Belgian Croix de Guerre; he had been a major-general since 1941 and was proud to have been one of Montgomery's most promising students. He had much of Montgomery's directness of approach and, as some of his officers were soon to discover, a good deal of his impatience and tactlessness. He was to prove himself a highly effective commander.

The Corps Commander, Major-General John P Lucas, was a man of a different stamp. He was fifty-four, and he felt, as he was to note in his diary on his birthday a few weeks later, 'every year of it'. He was patient, thorough, cautious, a friendly man with an unassuming manner, rarely to be seen without a corncob pipe – 'a pleasant, mild elderly gentleman', in the opinion of an officer in the Irish Guards who saw him for the first time before the landing being helped out of 'a layer of overcoats'.

Lucas had done well so far in the Italian campaign, acting at first as Eisenhower's personal representative between the headquarters in Northern Africa and the fighting troops, and then, after General Omar Bradley had gone to England to take over the First Army in preparation for Operation Overlord, as commander of II Corps. After Salerno he had been transferred to the command of VI Corps. He had never got on well with the British whom he did not altogether trust to perform the tasks allotted to them; and they in turn did not view him with anything like the favour they did the far less easy-going General Truscott.

After months of mountain warfare with VI Corps, the responsibilities of command had tired Lucas out. The entries in his diary reflect his growing lack of confidence, his concern for his troops, his worries about the future: 'I am far too tender-hearted ever to be a success at my chosen profession'; 'my subordinates do all the work and, most of the thinking'; 'I must keep from thinking of the fact that my order will send these men into a desperate attack . . . My constant prayer is that I may have the wisdom to bring them through this ordeal with the maximum of success and the minimum loss of life'; 'I can't see how our men stand what they do'; 'am running this thing on a shoe-string'; 'everything has gone to hell'.

The appointment to the Anzio command, although immediately reassuring to his failing confidence, soon increased the weight of his anxieties. Would he have enough time to prepare the plan? Would his men be given sufficient opportunities for training and rehearsal? Was there enough shipping available? Were not more men needed?

A conference on 9th January, presided over by the urbane and courteous Sir Harold Alexander, did nothing to assuage his fears. 'Sir Harold started the conference by stating that the operation would take place on January 22nd with the troops as scheduled and that there would be no more discussion on these points,' Lucas apprehensively recorded in his diary. 'He quoted Churchill as saying, "It will astonish the world", and added "it will certainly frighten Kesselring." I felt like a lamb being led to the slaughter but thought I was entitled to one bleat so I registered a protest against the target date as it gave me too little time for rehearsal. This is vital to the success of anything as terribly complicated as this. I was ruled down, as I knew I would be, many reasons being advanced as to the necessity for this speed...

'I have the bare minimum of ships and craft... The force that can be gotten ashore in a hurry is weak and I haven't sufficient artillery to hold me over...'

After the conference, Alexander tactfully confided to him, 'We have every confidence in you. That is why you were picked.' But in his memoirs, written when Lucas's performance at Anzio

Major-General John P Lucas, VI Corps commander, with corncob pipe

had disappointed the trust placed in him, Alexander gave a different reason for his selection: he was the only available Corps commander not actively engaged at the time.

Certainly, whoever had been appointed to the Anzio command would have had reason enough for anxiety. The time allowed for training and rehearsal was, as Lucas said, pitifully short; and, although the two divisions involved were, so he was blandly assured, experienced in amphibious operations, in fact the British 1st Division had met with no opposition during their landing on Pantelleria six months before and the American 3rd Division, heavily engaged since landing at Salerno, had lost the majority of its officers who had gained experience in fighting there. It was General Patton's belief that an amphibious operation required little training, anyway; and he had said as much to Lucas a few days before the invasion of Sicily. But Lucas felt strongly that more time ought to be allowed him; he was not fully aware of

how inextricably the time-table for Operation Shingle was tied to the time-table for Operation Overlord, and he saw his superiors' abrupt dismissal of his requests as a lack of sympathy for him in his problems.

Lucas's attitude to Operation Shingle became apparent to his divisional commanders and their staffs when they arrived at Caserta Palace north of Naples where the VI Corps had established its headquarters. It was clear to them that not only was there little optimism at Corps Headquarters as to the outcome of the operation, there was also as yet no firm plan for its conduct. All that seemed settled was that, with only two divisions, there could be no rapid advance towards the Alban Hills and across Route 6; there would have to be a steady build-up of resources in the beachhead to ensure the Corps' ability to withstand an early counter-attack. There must on no account be a repetition of what had happened at Salerno. Field Marshal Kesselring, the Commander-in-Chief in Italy, had plenty of reserves in the area of Rome and if they came down in force upon the two vulnerable Allied divisions straggled out from Anzio to the Alban Hills they might well succeed in driving them into the sea.

Yet further than insisting that no risks must be taken in the early stages of the Operation, General Lucas provided his divisional commanders with no plan of action within the scope of which their own orders might be framed. When General Penney asked for such a plan, he was given an operational instruction which merely reminded him that 'this directive does not include plans for an advance from the beachhead to or towards the final objective. Such plans are extremely tentative: this advance is not likely to take place unless it is synchronized with operations of the remainder of the Fifth Army in close vicinity of the beachhead'.

So there would in no circumstances be a quick advance from the beaches; nor would there be any commando raids; and, when the difficulties of employing paratroops had been examined, all idea of dropping the 504th Parachute Regiment beyond the beaches to secure important communications and commanding ground was abandoned. Beyond this Penney could gather virtually nothing of what his Division was intended to do after it had landed. Indeed he remained in ignorance when it was safely ashore, when it appeared to him a matter of vital importance to extend the limits of VI Corps' modest beachhead.

Lucas's caution was in striking contrast to the blithe assurance, the almost euphoric confidence of his superiors. 'Army has gone nuts again,' he recorded in exasperation in his diary. 'The general idea seems to be that the Germans are licked and are fleeing in disorder and nothing remains but to mop up. The only reason for such a belief is that we have recently been able

to advance a few miles against them with comparative ease. The Hun has pulled back a bit but I haven't seen the desperate fighting I have during the last four months without learning something. We are not (repeat not) in Rome yet... They will end up by putting me ashore with inadequate forces and get me into a serious jam. Then who will take the blame?'

But the 'higher-ups', as Lucas referred to them, seemed to believe that the Allies soon would be in Rome. Admiral Cunningham, the Commander-in-Chief in the Mediterranean, assured Lucas that the chances were 'seventy to thirty that by the time you reach Anzio, the Germans will be north of Rome'. General Alexander went so far as to suggest to him that the Anzio operation would probably make Operation Overlord unnecessary. 'I wish,' Lucas wrote with understandable resentment, 'that the higher-levels were not so over-optimistic.'

At least General Clark seemed to have less ambitious ideas about the early objectives of the operation. General Alexander, as Commander of the 15th Army Group, envisaged a quick capture

USS Biscayne, Lucas's command ship

of the Alban Hills after the seizure of the port of Anzio. But General Clark, as commander of one of the two armies comprising the 15th Army Group, emphasized to Lucas that his principal task was to gain and secure a beachhead. He must on no account press forward to the Alban Hills at the risk of losing his Corps. If there seemed no danger in getting onto the Alban Hills, all well and good; but his prime duty was to get his men ashore and to hold a beachhead.

These instructions, outlined in somewhat ambiguous terms in the Fifth Army's orders for Operation Shingle, were explained personally to Lucas by Clark's Chief Operations officer, Brigadier-General Donald W Brann, who made it clear to him that to Clark the beachhead was all-important, that the Alban Hills were not so much the objective of Lucas's VI Corps but of the remainder of the Fifth Army advancing up the Liri Valley. Yet if Operation Shingle caught the Germans completely off their guard and held promise of immediate success, Clark wanted to be able to profit by that too. He gave orders for the establishment of a Fifth Army command post close to Lucas's headquarters at Anzio once a beachhead had been secured. 'I wish to hell he wouldn't,' Lucas complained, 'I don't need any help.'

Determined to give Lucas as much help as was within his power, General Clark made available further troops for Operation Shingle a week before it was due to be launched. Already it had been decided that the two divisions and the 504th United States Parachute Regiment should be supported by the 509th United States Parachute Infantry Battalion, two British Commando battalions and three battalions of American Rangers. Now, in addition, Clark decided to give Lucas most of the 1st United States Armoured Division and a regiment of the 45th United States Division, as well as more artillery, for immediate reinforcements. If further reinforcements were required, the rest of the 1st Armoured and 45th Divisions would also be sent.

Commander of the 1st Armoured Division was Major-General Ernest N Harmon, a large, tough, outspoken, not

Above left: Major-General Ernest N Harmon, commander of United States 1st Armoured Division. *Above right:* Major-General William W Eagles, commander of 45th Division. *Right:* Major-General Lucian K Truscott, commander of 3rd Division

to say tactless and brusque, officer who had made many enemies during the course of his career but whose exceptional qualities were undoubted. The 45th Division's commander, Major-General William W Eagles was a quieter, less obtrusive man but quite as talented. In Lucas's opinion he was 'one of our most accomplished division commanders'. Lucas felt thankful that he was to have his support.

Indeed, despite Lucas's contention that he did not need any help when orders were given for the establishment of a Fifth Army Command post on the beachhead, he certainly felt the need of help in other forms when a rehearsal of the Anzio landing took place at Puzzuoli Bay near Naples on 19th January. For the rehearsal was a fiasco. Neither the naval forces, nor the American or British land forces involved came out of it with much credit. The British were 'incompetent' in one report, the Americans 'terrible' in another. An error in navigation led to the bigger transports stopping miles out to sea and to Rear Admiral Frank J Lowry of the United States Navy warning their captains that if they didn't

get closer inshore at Anzio they would all get 'a kick in a soft spot by a cruiser'. The LSTs let down their doors too soon; many valuable pieces of equipment, including ten howitzers, were lost; several men were drowned; forty DUKWs sank.

Both Clark and Truscott displayed their fury at this demonstration of ineptitude; and Lucas asked for more time so that another rehearsal could take place. But there was no time to spare; the landing craft had to be returned for Operation Overlord by the required date; there could be no second rehearsal.

'You won't get another rehearsal,' Clark told Lucas bluntly. 'The date has been set at the very highest level. There is no possibility of delaying it even for a day. You've got to do it.'

The whole affair, Lucas decided despondently, had a strong odour of Gallipoli. In fact, he confided to Admiral Cunningham that he thought it was going to be 'worse than Gallipoli'. 'If that's how you feel about it,' Cunningham replied without much sympathy, 'you had better resign.'

But Lucas had no thought of resign-

The Allies 'crawl up the leg like a harvest bug' as Churchill put it, during their Italian advance. *Above:* DUKWs on the Eighth Army Front
Right: British troops cross the Garigliano

ing. He knew he would not get more men and more time if he threatened to do so; and, in any case, his sense of duty was too strong. Besides, although he had 'many misgivings' which continually found their way on to the pages of his diary, he was 'also optimistic'. He thought he stood a good chance to 'make a killing'; and if the weather held good, he felt he would be 'all right'.

Much depended, of course, upon the course of the Fifth Army's attack on the Gustav Line. If it pinned the Germans down along the Line and drew in reinforcements to support them there – if, even better, it succeeded in breaking through the Line and the Allies burst out into the Liri Valley – all would be well.

First reports of the Fifth Army's advance were encouraging. The French Expeditionary Corps, on the right of the Army's line along the upper reaches of the Rapido River, opened the attack on 12th January. In terrible weather and appallingly difficult country, they

managed to advance several miles. Three days later the American II Corps, in the centre of the line, advanced to capture Monte Trocchio which commanded the approaches to the Rapido. On 17th January, the British on the left attacked across the upper Garigliano and, with the help of LCTs and DUKWs, succeeded in establishing a bridgehead north of the river not far from its mouth.

But, having got so far, the Fifth Army could get no further. The British failed both to extend their bridgehead and to establish another one closer to the Americans on their right. The Americans, attempting to get across the Rapido in darkness and fog on 20th January, were repulsed with heavy losses: the 36th (Texan) Division suffered over 1,500 casualties. Hopes of quickly breaking through the Gustav Line and into the Liri Valley were dashed; and Operation Shingle would have to be launched in the knowledge that a rapid link up with the rest of the Fifth Army was no longer possible.

On 20th January, the day that the American 36th Division was to begin its ordeal on the banks of the Rapido, General Lucas went aboard the *USS Biscayne*. He was not feeling well, and the assurances that the Fifth Army attacks would suck many German troops to the south did not comfort him. 'The high command seems to think they will stay there,' he wrote. 'I don't see why. They can slow us up there and move against me at the same time.' A visit from General Patton had done nothing to cheer him up.

'John, there is no one in the army I'd hate to see get killed as much as you, but you can't get out of this alive,' Patton grimly assured him. 'Of course, you might get wounded. No one ever blames a wounded general!' To one of

Lucas's staff, Patton added the advice, 'If things get too bad, shoot the old man in the backside!'

General Truscott, commander of the American 3rd Division, was scarcely more confident. He came aboard the *Biscayne* to the loud strains of his Division's signature tune, played by the Divisional band, its words defiantly sung by the troops on board: 'I'm just a dog-faced soldier with a rifle on my shoulder, and I eat a Kraut for breakfast every day...' But Truscott, while keeping his apprehensions to himself could not share these sentiments.

As he had written to Major-General Alfred M Gruenther, Clark's Chief of Staff, 'I believe that you know me well enough to know that I would not make such a point unless I actually felt *strongly* about it. If this is to be a "forlorn hope" or "suicide sashay" then all I want to know is that fact – If so, I'm positive that there is no outfit in the world that can do it better than me – even though I reserve the right (person-

Left: Sherman in an awkward situation
Above: Supplies are ferried ashore at
Anzio beach

ally) to believe we might deserve a better fate.'

There were, of course, numerous minor worries. For to organise the transport of thirty thousand men and over five thousand vehicles more than a hundred miles to an enemy-occupied coastline, to keep them adequately supplied and reinforced, and to keep the whole operation secret, was a formidable undertaking. The difficulties of supply were emphasized not only by the different weapons and ammunitions, the different vehicles and spare parts of the two divisions involved, but also by the continuing shortage of LSTs. To some extent these difficulties were overcome by a plan devised at Corps Headquarters which provided for trucks, already loaded with supplies, to be driven straight off the LSTs on to the beach and up to the appropriate dumps, empty trucks being driven on to the LSTs for the return journey. For some reason this plan was not approved by the higher authorities to whom it

was submitted; but VI Corps ignored the ban, and the system was to work in practice with considerable success.

As well as the problem of using the LSTs to the best advantage there was also the problem of keeping their ultimate destination secret. Although enemy reconnaissance aircraft rarely now got through the Allied defences, it was obviously impossible to keep the assembly of an armada of 374 ships entirely hidden from German Intelligence. And although various cover plans were devised it was impossible to be sure that the enemy was being deceived by any of them. Bombardments from the sea and the air, flights of reconnaissance aircraft, the broadcasting of false orders and messages, were all intended to persuade the enemy that a landing was being planned north of Rome in the area of Civitavecchia, yet when a team of naval officers, surveying the coastline around Anzio by night in rubber dinghies, failed to return, it was feared that they had been captured and the Allies' intentions made known.

With fears such as this in his mind, General Lucas anxiously awaited the time for the convoy to set sail.

The landing

'As I traversed the front I had the confident feeling that the Allies had missed a uniquely favourable chance of capturing Rome.' Field Marshal Kesselring on the situation at Anzio on the afternoon of 22nd January 1944.

On 21st January, in perfect weather, the great assault convoys set sail from the Bay of Naples under a cloud of barrage balloons. The American officer in command was Rear-Admiral Lowry. Commanding the British Task Force was Rear-Admiral T H Troubridge. In the convoys there were cruisers and gunboats, destroyers and minesweepers, tugs and trawlers, submarines and hospital ships, AA ships

and HQ ships, motor launches and scout craft, as well as the various and numerous landing craft for tanks and infantry. Of the 374 craft, 210 were British, 157 American, four Greek, two Dutch and one Polish.

It seemed to many soldiers aboard too much to hope that this vast armada would not be spotted by the enemy. But heavy bombing of the airfields in central Italy kept reconnaissance aircraft grounded, while a comprehensive cover plan had drawn the Germans' attention away from the coast line south of Rome to areas further north.

Troops and landing-craft had been assembled in Corsica and Sardinia; a radio station had been set up to transmit messages purporting to come from a corps headquarters well to the north of Rome; a naval force had been instructed to bombard Civitavecchia where coastal craft were to be collected to make dummy landings. Terracina and Leghorn were also to be bombarded; and air attacks were to be made on targets that suggested landings were about to take place not only north of Rome but even in the south of France.

So no reconnaissance aircraft were seen in the clear skies over the Bay of Naples that day, and no German bombers appeared to disrupt the calm passage of the convoys. To deceive any malevolent onlookers who might be watching from the shore, and to avoid the German minefields, the ships turned south outside the Bay; but when darkness fell they were steaming north for Anzio.

At midnight the assault ships hove to, and, while minesweepers cleared the channels, the assault craft were swung out and the landing ships chugged into position closer towards the shore. Shortly before two o'clock in the morning opposite each of the three landing points, the rocket ships sent over two thousand 5-inch rockets hurtling on to the beaches where for five

LSTs are loaded at Naples for the Anzio landing

41

Support for the Fifth Army from the
Twelfth Air Force: a Boston takes
evasive action after its bomb run

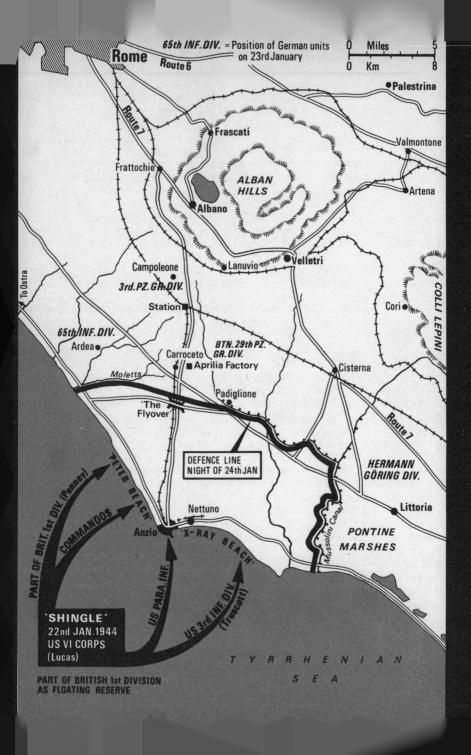

Rome

65th INF. DIV. = Position of German units on 23rd January

Route 6

0 — Miles — 5
0 — Km — 8

• Palestrina

Route 7

• Frascati

Frattochie

ALBAN HILLS

• Albano

• Valmontone

• Artena

Campoleone

3rd. PZ. GR. DIV.

• Lanuvio   • Velletri

COLLI LEPINI

Station ■

• Cori

To Ostra

65th INF. DIV.

Ardea •

Carroceto •   BTN. 29th PZ. GR. DIV.
            ■ Aprilia Factory

Moletta

• Cisterna

Route 7

Padiglione •

'The Flyover'

DEFENCE LINE NIGHT OF 24th JAN

HERMANN GÖRING DIV.

Nettuno •

Mussolini Canal

• Littoria

PETER BEACH

COMMANDOS

PART OF BRIT. 1st DIV (Penney)

Anzio •

'X-RAY BEACH'

US PARA. INF.

US 3rd INF. DIV. (Truscott)

PONTINE MARSHES

'SHINGLE'
22nd JAN. 1944
US VI CORPS
(Lucas)

PART OF BRITISH 1st DIVISION
AS FLOATING RESERVE

T Y R R H E N I A N
S E A

minutes they exploded with their deafening and characteristically explosive crack. When all was quiet again the first wave of the assault went in.

There were difficulties, of course: the rockets had not detonated all the mines on the beaches, while the British beaches themselves, with a gradient of 1:120 and composed of a soft sand, were the worst that Admiral Troubridge had encountered in his whole experience. Yet the landing was remarkably successful. Almost complete tactical surprise had been achieved; the enemy were nowhere to be seen. Occasionally a self-propelled gun opened fire from the woods, but otherwise the troops poured ashore unmolested. Two Brigade Groups of General Penney's 1st British Division, together with two battalions of Commandos (the 9th and 43rd) landed about five miles north of Anzio on what was known as 'Peter Beach'. The American 3rd Division, under General Truscott, landed four miles south of the town on 'X-Ray Beach'; while three battalions of American Rangers, the 504th American Parachute Infantry Regiment and the 509th Parachute Infantry Battalion, assaulted Anzio itself and occupied Nettuno. The remainder of the 1st Division was held as a floating reserve; while General Ernest N Harmon's 1st American Armoured Division and General William W Eagles's 45th American Infantry Division were also to be held in reserve as follow-up troops.

By 0800 hours on 22nd January, the port at Anzio, from which the Germans had evacuated the civilian population, was safely in American hands and nine hours later landing ships and landing craft were coming in to unload guns and heavy equipment. By then the British troops from 'Peter Beach' and the Americans from 'X-Ray Beach' had long since made contact behind Anzio and had established a single and substantial beachhead.

The British were across the coastal road that ran from Anzio, over the Motella river and up to Ardea and Ostia. The Americans had reached the Mussolini Canal, a barrier 240 feet wide between high embankments, which was to form the flank protection of the beachhead to the south. Within less than twenty-four hours of the first landings, more than 36,000 men had walked ashore. In the entire Corps, which had taken 227 prisoners, there were only 154 men killed, wounded or missing. The one serious disappointment was that the shallow, soft British 'Peter Beach' had to be closed, all unloading operations being transferred to Anzio which was already overcrowded. Nevertheless, by early morning on 23rd January over three thousand vehicles and immense stores of equipment were safely inside the beachhead.

A captured German officer, who had been despatched to Anzio with a small detachment of men to render the port useless, watched the Americans at work on 'Peter Beach' and he could not but admire their efficiency. 'Every man knew his place and his job,' he said. There was no 'confusion, disorder or muddle'. He was amazed by the amount of equipment that was being brought so quickly ashore. There were even bulldozers at work, levelling the slope of the beach, making tracks which were soon surfaced with wire netting.

Apart from some largely ineffectual long-range shelling from the Alban Hills, a quickly silenced resistance from some coast artillery and anti-aircraft units, and a brief raid on the harbour by six Messerschmitt dive bombers that managed to penetrate the ack-ack screen protecting the fleet, there had been virtually no opposition to the landing. General Lucas wrote in his diary, 'We achieved what is certainly one of the most complete surprises in history. The *Biscayne* was anchored three and a half miles off shore, and I could not believe my eyes when I stood on the bridge and saw no machine-gun or other fire on the beach'. He sent a message to General Clark informing him that the landings had been successful and that the subsequent

Above: The Scots Guards embark. *Below:* DUKWs are loaded at Salerno harbour

advances of the 1st and 3rd Divisions were going well.

Thus heartened, Clark and Alexander set off for Anzio to survey the encouraging situation for themselves. They landed in a speed boat, and Alexander was soon driving in a jeep through the British sector with Admiral Troubridge. He expressed himself as 'very satisfied', and later told Lucas that he had done 'a splendid piece of work'. 'Before I left,' he recorded in his memoirs, 'I felt confident that VI Corps were sufficiently established to push forward light mobile forces to gain contact with any German forces in the vicinity.' That evening he cabled to Churchill: 'We appear to have got almost complete surprise. I have stressed the importance of strong-hitting mobile patrols being boldly pushed out to gain contact with the enemy, but so far have not received reports of their activities.' Churchill replied, 'Thank you for all your messages. I am very glad you are pegging out claims rather than digging in beachheads.'

The position on the beachhead, however, was far more static than either Alexander intended or Churchill believed. For Lucas was determined not to be held responsible for another Salerno. He deemed it essential to keep his troops well in hand, to maintain a strong reserve under Corps command. He had even kept General Penney at sea for several hours after Anzio had been taken, refusing him permission to join the units of his Division now securely established ashore. Any moment, Lucas feared, he would be under heavy attack by German tanks, perhaps by the tanks of the 29th and 90th Panzer Grenadiers which had been reported by his Intelligence Staff as being held in reserve in the vicinity of Rome. Predisposed to be cautious, he had, in any case, been warned by Clark not to stick his neck out. 'I did at Salerno,' Clark told him, 'and got into trouble.' 'You can,' Clark had added, 'forget this goddam Rome business.'

Lucas was very glad to forget it. Ignoring the opportunity which the situation presented to him of sending out strong-hitting mobile patrols up into the Alban Hills and so cutting across the road and rail communications to the Cassino front, he concentrated on securing his tightly-knit Corps Beachhead Line, his determination to do so reinforced by Clark's orders. These were so worded, Lucas noted with gratification, 'so as not to force me to push on, at the risk of sacrificing my Corps'.

Yet if he had pushed on, there would have been no question of sacrificing his Corps. Far from there being strong Panzer formations in the area, in the early hours of the Allied attack there were but few scattered and weak units which could have been brought immediately into action in defence of the capital. Near Anzio there was an under-strength battalion of the 29th Panzer Grenadier Division which had been withdrawn for a rest; near Cisterna there were the remains of a battered tank regiment and some artillery from the Hermann Göring Division, also withdrawn for a rest. And that was all.

Field Marshal Kesselring had been caught completely off-guard. It was not that he had disregarded the possibility of an Allied landing on the Tyrrhenian coast. Indeed, he had taken the precaution of holding strong reserves to deal with such a landing whenever it might fall; and careful preparations had been made so that the routes to all of the five areas most likely to be attacked were kept open, free of ice, and supplied with fuel; while pontoons were held ready in case Allied air attacks destroyed vital bridges. The troops to fight off the Allied threat were to come from the 14th Army in the north of Italy, or, if necessary, from the Balkans or the South of France. And, in addition to these, as a mobile force closer at hand, two divisions, the 111st Panzer Grenadier and the Hermann Göring Divisions, had been withdrawn from the Tenth Army on the Cassino front.

When the Fifth Army made their attack along the Garigliano, however,

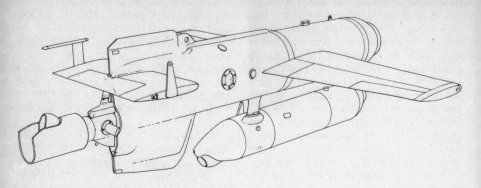

The Germans had always shown the greatest interest in developing new sorts of weapon, and in the field of guided missiles they were far ahead of the Allies. One of the earliest German guided missiles to go into service was the Henschel Hs 293, which was launched from a parent aircraft and then steered onto its target by radio. It scored several successes at Anzio, where it was used by KG 100. The missile's Walter rocket motor developed a maximum thrust of 1,250 pounds, which gave the weapon a speed of 375 mph over a maximum range of 10 miles. Its warhead weighed 725 pounds and the all up weight at launch was 2,870 pounds. Span was 9.5 feet, length 11.7 feet and body diameter 1.6 feet

General Heinrich von Vietinghoff *gennant* Scheel, the Tenth Army commander, urgently asked for the return of these two divisions, warning Kesselring that, if he did not get them, his right wing would be driven in. After what Kesselring's Chief of Staff, General Siegfried Westphal, described as 'a bitter tussle over the disposition of the two divisions', Kesselring agreed to let them go. He was assured by his Intelligence staff that an Allied landing would not take place for at least another four weeks, while Westphal also considered 'a large scale landing operation as being out of the question for the next four to six weeks'. Kesselring himself recognised that the new threat to the Gustav Line was 'the greatest threat yet encountered'; the whole fate of the Tenth Army hung by a slender thread. So von Vietinghoff's demands were met; he was granted the two divisions, together with the headquarters of I Parachute Corps to assist him in controlling

his enlarged force. The decision was made on 18th January, three days before Operation Shingle began.

The correctness of Kesselring's fateful decision seemed to be confirmed when Admiral Canaris, Chief of Intelligence in Berlin, arrived at his headquarters. Canaris was consulted on the possibility of an Allied landing behind the Gustav Line to coincide with the attacks on the Cassino front. There was 'not the slightest sign' of it, Canaris told Kesselring's staff; shipping in the port at Naples was reported to be 'quite normal'.

Although still not entirely convinced that an Allied landing did not remain a possibility, Kesselring allowed himself to be persuaded that the danger was receding. When the Cassino attack began he had ordered all units to stand-to; but the troops were now getting tired, they badly needed a rest. And Kesselring reluctantly decided that they should be given one. They were granted permission to stand down on the night of 21st January, the very night of Operation Shingle.

But as soon as he received the report of a fighter pilot who had been sent out on patrol and realised the seriousness of the threat at Anzio, Kesselring reacted with characteristic speed. He realised immediately that he must at all costs not only hold the Alban Hills, but also prevent the Allies pushing past Velletri and on to Route 6. He gave orders for all available troops, including those from base camps and rest areas, to take up positions without a moment's delay along Route 7. At the same time he despatched as many anti-aircraft batteries as were available in the Rome area under General Ritter von Pohl with instructions for them to act as anti-tank batteries in building a cordon of guns around the beachhead. General Schlemmer, Commander of I Parachute Corps, was ordered to bring every man he could into the line to strengthen this cordon and prevent the enemy from breaking through it. Kesselring told Schlemmer 'to push all units as they arrived as far south as possible so as to help the flak slow down or halt the enemy advance. 'Every yard,' Kesselring emphasized in his memoirs, 'was important to me.'

Men were summoned from no less than eight different divisions; they came from the Gustav Line and from behind it, from Rimini, Genoa, Perugia and Leghorn; others were soon on the way from Yugoslavia and even the South of France and Germany. 'It was a higgledy-piggledy jumble', Kesselring said afterwards, 'units of numerous divisions fighting confusedly side by side.' And as he left for the front to impress upon these units the danger of the situation, he could not but doubt that the reinforcements would arrive in time. Already staff officers were packing bags and burning papers in Rome where Allied planes had dropped thousands of leaflets informing the people of the landing. Surely soon the news would come that Cisterna or Campoleone had fallen, that the enemy

were on the road to Albano, that a flying column had reached the suburbs of Rome. For, as General Westphal said, 'the road to Rome was open, and an audacious flying column could certainly have penetrated to the city'. In Kesselring's own words, there was 'a uniquely favourable chance of capturing Rome and opening the door on the Garigliano front'. Vietinghoff, indeed, believed that now so many troops had been taken away from him he 'could not possibly' hold the Cassino front and advised a withdrawal until the Anzio beachhead had been contained.

But to Westphal's amazement and to Kesselring's profound relief, the Allies 'remained astonishingly passive' at Anzio. They showed no sign of breaking out of their beachhead. And by the end of the morning of 22nd January, although his staff, in Westphal's words, remained in 'a state of acute continuous tension', Kesselring himself 'already had the feeling that the worst danger had been staved off'. The Allies had missed their opportunity and time was now on his side. A German report concluded that the 'Allies on the beachhead on the first day of the landing did not conform to the German High Command's expectations. Instead of moving northward with the first wave to seize the Alban Hills... the landing forces limited their objectives... Their initial action was to occupy a small beachhead ... As the Allied forces made no preparations for a large-scale attack on the first day of the landings, the German command estimated that the Allies would improve their positions, and bring up more troops... During this time sufficient German troops would arrive to prevent an Allied breakthrough.'

By the evening of 23rd January, when the Allies had made no attempt to expand the beachhead, Kesselring felt able to assure Vietinghoff that 'the danger of a large-scale expansion was no longer imminent'.

As time wore on and still the Allies did not move, the hastily improvised cordon began to assume a more orderly

shape and to gain a formidable strength. 'On 22nd January and even the following day, an audacious and enterprising formation of enemy troops . . . could have penetrated into the city of Rome itself without having to overcome any serious opposition,' General Westphal wrote afterwards. 'But the landed enemy forces lost time and hesitated.' And now it was too late for them to hope for a quick dash to the Alban Hills.

The 3rd Panzer Grenadier Division, which had been en route to the Adriatic front, was in position opposite the British near Campoleone, while the 65th Infantry Division from Genoa was organising a system of defences beyond the Moletta. Opposite the Americans, between Cisterna and Littoria, was the Hermann Göring Division which had been brought back from the Garigliano. Other units either in the area, or soon to be on their way once the fighting along the Gustav Line began to die down, were elements of the 15th Panzer Grenadier Division from Cassino, of the 4th Parachute Division from Perugia, the 26th Panzer Grenadiers

from the Adriatic, the 362nd Infantry Division from Rimini, the 715th (Motorized) Infantry Division from the South of France and the 114th Jäger Division from Yugoslavia. The Allied air forces did what they could to prevent their movements taking place. Heavy and medium bombers bombed road and rail communications; but flying conditions after 24th January seriously reduced the effectiveness of the raids. In any case the Germans had long since grown accustomed to moving by night and were expert in the speedy repair of damaged bridges. Placed in overall control of the Anzio area on 22nd January was General Schlemmer, the headquarters of whose 1st Parachute Corps had arrived from the Garigliano front.

The night after General Schlemmer's appointment to the Anzio command, the Luftwaffe made a damaging attack on the shipping in the harbour. Already the quays and the anchorages had been subjected to intermittent shelling; now dive-bombers came into the attack on the crowded shipping with aerial torpedoes and the newly invented radio-controlled glider-bombs, armour-piercing bombs weighing about 2,500 pounds, which had proved so effective at Salerno. The Allied navies had learned how to deflect these glider-bombs by jamming or bending the radio beam, and destroyers had been equipped with special apparatus to detect bombs and pull them harmlessly off target. But occasionally a skilful German could keep the bomb on its course; and on 23rd January one bomb escaped the Allied net and sank the British destroyer *Janus*. Later the hospital ship, *St David,* although illuminated in accordance with the code of the International Red Cross, was also hit and sunk.

There was a further heavy air raid the next day, for Hitler had personally ordered the Luftwaffe to strike with all its force at Anzio, to bomb the troops and to attack the shipping in the harbour. There was to have been a further raid on the 25th but that day the

Left: American Army engineers clear the beach by exploding captured mines. *Above:* Troops climb down into Higgins boats for reinforcement landings on 26th January. *Below:* A quiet beach on the American sector, as General Lucas concentrates on building up supplies

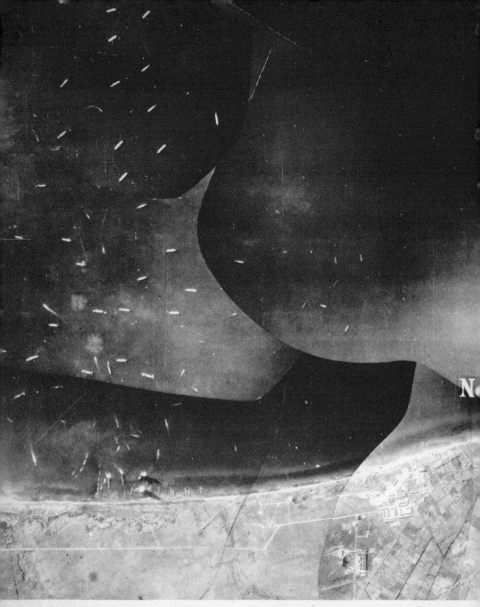

Composite photograph of Anzio area at about 10.30 am on the morning of the assault. The 3rd Infantry Division landing beach is at bottom left

weather broke, the wind got up and soon gales were howling across the harbour. The sea was in ferment, pontoons broke loose, ships were driven on shore and, although the port was spared the attentions of the Luftwaffe, all unloading had to be suspended. On the 26th, however, unloading began again; and so, too, did the bombing. When the raid ended that day the damage to Allied shipping was already severe.

But already by the late afternoon of the 23rd vast quantities of stores had been unloaded, and the first of the follow-up forces, units of the American 1st Armoured Division and the 179th

Anzio

ttuno

Regimental Combat Team of the American 45th Infantry Division, had come ashore. Yet General Lucas was still far more concerned with the consolidation of the beachhead than with any forceful move out of it. 'I must keep my feet on the ground,' he cautioned himself in his diary, 'and keep my forces in hand and do nothing foolish. This is the most important thing I have ever tried to do and I will not be stampeded.' He had learned from his Intelligence staff that 40,000 Germans had already moved into the Anzio area and that Hitler had issued a special Order of the Day: 'The Gustav Line must be held at all costs for the sake of the political consequences following upon the successful defence of it. The Führer expects the most bitter struggle for every yard.' Lucas read the messages with self-confessed apprehension.

Above: Rear-Admiral Frolov (left) of the Russian Navy acting as observer on the amphibious operation with Rear-Admiral Troubridge of the Royal Navy.

Above and below: Rough seas during the gales of 25th January *Below left:*
Build-up for the British 1st Division on Peter Beach

Destroyer smoke screen for supply shipping

Top : The Luftwaffe replies with attacks on the assembled shipping. *Centre :* The town of Nettuno comes under bomb attack. *Bottom :* Not even the hospital ships were immune

Allied guns reply to a German night air
attack

The Allies attack

'All efforts should now be concentrated on full-scale co-ordinated attacks to capture Cisterna and Campoleone followed by a rapid attack on Velletri.' General the Hon Sir Harold Alexander to Lieutenant-General Mark W Clark, 27th January 1944.

For all his anxiety not to take any risks, General Lucas could not but accept the fact that he would be compelled to try to push the Germans back a little, if only to give his increasingly constricted force more room in which to move.

By the night of 24th January the Corps beachhead line was still limited by the Mussolini Canal in the south, and the Moletta in the north. Neither the little town of Cisterna, which dominated the route to Velletri in front of the

Americans, nor the railway station at Campoleone, which was the key to an advance on Albano, had yet been included in the perimeter, although both these important centres of communication could have been taken without effort in the early hours of the landing. Now both were strongly defended, and would not be easily taken. Yet if the beachhead were to be expanded successfully, they would both *have* to be taken.

Now that a substantial part of the follow-up troops had arrived so that most of the 1st Division could be released from the Corps reserve, there was no longer any excuse for delay in at least preparing for an attack. General Lucas authorised General Penney to send out an exploratory patrol towards Campoleone, and General Truscott to take the German defences around Cisterna.

The road that led up from Anzio through the British lines towards Campoleone and the Alban Hills went under two flyover bridges. The first of these bridges, just the other side of the Padiglione Woods on the edge of the British perimeter, carried a narrow side road over the main road and became known to the troops as the 'Flyover Bridge'. The second bridge, which became known as 'The Embankment', carried over the road a disused railway track.

Early on the morning of 24th January, a patrol of Grenadier Guards from the 24th Guards Brigade, riding in Bren-gun carriers, drove through these two bridges in the first patrol that had so far left the British lines. They passed through the first bridge safely, and drove on towards the little village of Carroceto, the electric railway line from Rome to Anzio running parallel to the road on their left.

A few Italians could be seen in the fields and outside the farm cottages on both sides of the road, but otherwise there was no sign of life. The Guards

25-pounder crew fires on German positions

passed under the second bridge, beneath the cinders of the disused railway track, and then came out in sight of the railway station at Campoleone, the Alban Hills to the north, and, closer at hand, the little village of Carroceto, now less than a hundred yards away.

On the edge of the village was a new, red-brick farm settlement known as Aprilia – just such a one as several others that the Fascists had built in the recently reclaimed Pontine Marshes. There were flats and shops, offices and a community centre, a church and a doctor's surgery. But to the Grenadiers it looked more like a factory; and as 'The Factory' it was thereafter known.

It was from the area of 'The Factory' that the Grenadiers, who had by now travelled some four miles up the road towards Campoleone, were first fired upon by a self-propelled gun. At the same moment, from the other side of the road, they were brought under heavy small-arms fire.

The carriers wheeled round and drove back fast down the road. When General Penney received the Grenadiers' report he sought permission to attack 'The Factory'. General Lucas was reluctant to risk a compromising advance against what might prove to be a strongly held position; but eventually during the afternoon of the 24th, he granted his consent. The Guards received orders to move against 'The Factory' at half-past seven the following morning, while the 2nd Brigade covered their left flank by an advance in the direction of Ardea.

The Guards had to fight hard to take 'The Factory'. In prolonged and vicious hand-to-hand fighting they suffered many casualties; and no sooner had they occupied it than they had to withstand a counterattack by the 29th Panzer Grenadiers. It was painfully clear that a continued advance to Campoleone would be a very serious undertaking.

The Americans in their advance towards Cisterna had come across equally strong resistance from the Hermann Göring Division, finding that every important building in front of them was now occupied by the enemy and protected by self-propelled guns. To advance on this axis was going to be quite as difficult as to advance towards the Alban Hills.

In both Armies puzzled and increasingly frustrated soldiers asked themselves why there had been this long delay before any attempts had been made to push forward inland. The days of waiting may have allowed great quantities of supplies to build up in and around Anzio and Nettuno; but with every hour the capacity of German resistance had grown and continued to grow. Shelling, too, was becoming heavier, and a formidable 280mm railroad gun was now in position near Velletri. Known to the troops as 'Anzio Annie' or the 'Anzio Express', it rumbled out of a tunnel, fired a few shells across the Allied lines and then backed away into safety. Air raids were not yet as frequent as they were to become later, since the Luftwaffe was concentrating on the port, but they were already causing considerable damage and fraying the men's nerves. The unpleasant weather, the reports of further setbacks at Cassino, the realisation that heavy casualties at Anzio were now all but inevitable, all added to the darkening mood.

It was a mood shared to the full by General Lucas. 'I am doing my best,' he noted in his diary on 25th January, 'but it seems terribly slow.' 'This waiting is terrible,' he recorded the next day. 'I want an all-out Corps effort but the time hasn't come yet and the weather will not help matters. Bad for tanks. I might be able to move soon,' but not before the whole of the 45th Division had been landed.

Progress was, indeed, terribly slow; and both Churchill and Alexander were becoming seriously concerned. 'We have launched the big attack against the German armies defending Rome which I told you about at Teheran,' Churchill had cabled to Stalin on 21st January. 'The weather conditions seem favourable. I hope to have good news

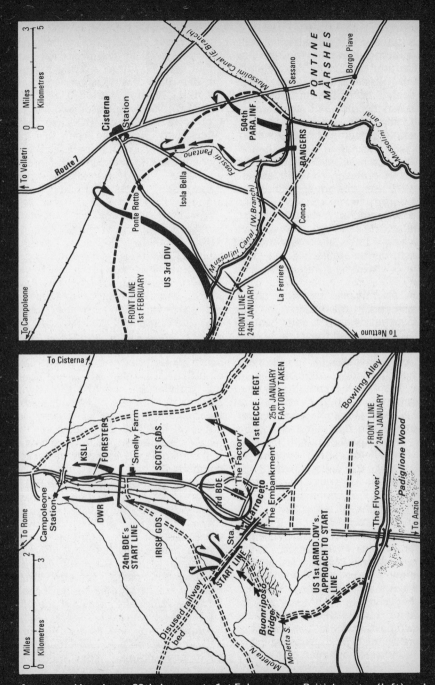

Attempted breakout, 29th January to 1st February, on British sector (left) and American sector (right)

for you before long.' But after the initial success of the landings, there had been nothing further to report. On 28th January, Churchill cabled to Alexander, 'It would be unpleasant if your troops were sealed off there and the main army could not advance up from the south.' Alexander had no need to be reminded of how unpleasant this eventuality would prove to be; and he had already impressed his anxiety upon Mark Clark, ordering him on 27th January 'to press the advance with the utmost energy before the enemy reinforcements could arrive'. He suggested 'that all efforts should now be concentrated on full-scale co-ordinated attacks to capture Cisterna and Campoleone followed by a rapid attack on Velletri'.

Soon after receiving Alexander's communication, Clark left for the beachhead in a motor torpedo boat. As the boat approached the channel leading to the port an American minesweeper opened fire on it in the half light and Clark was nearly killed. He arrived at Lucas's headquarters in an anxious frame of mind. 'Beachhead progress was lagging unnecessarily,' he commented later and he urged Lucas, whose plans seemed far from clear, to 'speed up his attack towards Cisterna, a town we wanted in our defensive line.'

'Apparently some of the higher levels think I have not advanced with maximum speed,' Lucas wrote sadly in his diary after Clark had gone, recording his own appreciation of the situation. 'I think more has been accomplished than anyone had a right to expect. This venture was always a desperate one and I could never see much chance for it to succeed, if success means driving the Germans north of Rome. The one factor that has allowed us to get established ashore has been the port of Anzio. Without it our situation by this time would have been desperate with little chance

The town of Anzio, 'softened' by Allied bombing strikes in anticipation of heavy resistance

Known to the Germans as 'Slim
Bertha', but by the Allies as 'Anzio
Annie', the 28cm railway gun used by
the Germans at Anzio was one of the
War's most potent pieces of artillery.
It was hidden in a tunnel for most of
the time, emerging only to fire its
561 pound shell at the Allied beachhead.
The weight of the gun and its railway
carriage was 479,600 pounds, and its
length was 96 feet. Its maximum range,
with the 561 pound shell, was 66,880
yards (38 miles), and its firing crew
numbered ten

The American 105mm howitzer, which was very easy to handle, was one of the Allies most favoured weapons, and many conversions of tanks and other vehicles were made so that this weapon could be fitted, with a consequent improvement in its mobility. One of the more interesting conversions was its fitting onto a White Half-Track, shown here. The howitzer had a range of 12,500 yards and a rate of fire of four rounds per minute. The White Half-Track had a maximum speed of 45 mph and a range of 210 miles

of a build-up to adequate strength. As it is, we are doing well and, in addition to troops, unloaded over four thousand tons of supplies yesterday.

'Had I been able to rush to the high ground around Albano... immediately upon landing, nothing would have been accomplished except to weaken my force... because the troops sent, being completely beyond supporting distance, would have been immediately destroyed. The only thing to do was what I did. Get a proper beachhead and prepare to hold it. Keep the enemy off balance by a constant advance against him by small units, not committing anything as large as a division until the Corps was ashore and everything was set. Then make a co-ordinated attack to defeat the enemy and seize the objective...

'There has been no chance, with available shipping, to build "Shingle" up to a decisive strength and anyone with any knowledge of logistics could have seen that from the start. I have done what I was ordered to do, desperate though it was. I can win if I am let alone but I don't know whether I can stand the strain of having so many people looking over my shoulders.'

On 29th January, however, Lucas agreed that he had now built up sufficient strength to launch a major attack. For this 'major effort', Lucas had available 70,000 men, 27,000 tons of stores and over five hundred guns. There were also 237 tanks, for the greater part of the American 1st Armoured Division was now ashore.

It was decided that the advance out of the beachhead should take the form of a two-pronged attack – an attack by the Americans on Cisterna and across Highway 7 so as to be in a position to continue the advance towards Velletri, and an attack by the British on Campoleone railway station to gain both ground and base for a subsequent advance to Albano. The British attack was to be supported by the tanks of the American 1st Armoured Division which were to drive round Campoleone in a sweeping curve to their left. The American attack was to be made by the 3rd Division, supported by the 504th Parachute Regiment and the Rangers.

'I remember the general air of hurry and uncertainty that surrounded all plan making at Anzio,' wrote Wynford Vaughan-Thomas, the BBC's war correspondent in his excellent first-hand account of the battle. 'I think of the last-minute conferences before the maps at Corps HQ in the bleak, bare house in Nettuno – meetings which, in General Truscott's opinion, too often turned into debates; of the arguments between divisional generals about ground and the hurried radio messages summoning worried colonels to report to brigades for briefings; above all, of how totally pointless accidents can cause tragic and unexpected delays.'

There was one such accident before the Allied attack which caused a fatal delay.

The 24th Guards Brigade had been assigned the task of securing a lateral road that crossed the main road and the Rome-Anzio railway line between 'The Factory' and Campoleone station. This road was to serve as the start line for the attack, a clearly defined line which would ensure a tidy start and serve as an unmistakable reference for artillery and supporting troops.

In the final stages of planning their part in the forthcoming operation, the company commanders of the Grenadier Guards left for a conference with their fellow officers of the Scots Guards. The driver of the jeep in which they were travelling to the headquarters of the Scots Guards took the wrong turning and drove into the German lines. The jeep was destroyed and all the officers were shot.

There was no alternative but to delay the attack. The role assigned to the Grenadiers had now to be given to the Irish Guards; and, since it was essential that the British and American attacks were co-ordinated, General Truscott's advance had also to be delayed. The delay, which lasted for twenty-four

German troops plant anti-tank mines

hours, allowed the Germans to increase their strength still further, to improve the defences of the soundly built farm-houses all along their front, to build mine-fields, site machine-guns and bring up more tanks. Indeed, had it not been for the Allied air strikes on their communications, the Germans themselves would have advanced against the beachhead. A provisional date, 28th January, had already been set for their counteroffensive which obviously would not be delayed much longer if the Allied attack did not soon go in.

At last, on the night of 29th January, the Allied attack did go in. On the left, two companies of the Irish Guards and the Scots Guards moved up towards the start line in the darkness, at first in silence, then behind a ferocious artil-lery barrage. They needed all the pro-tection from the artillery they could get, for the Germans had occupied Campoleone in large numbers. Mach-ine-guns, self-propelled guns, the guns

of tanks fired at them unremittingly, causing such heavy casualties that when they did manage to get forward to the track which was their objective, it seemed doubtful that they would be able to hold it. Certainly, when daylight came, they would not be able to hold it against tanks unless their own tanks came through to support them.

The tanks available to support them were very few; and the commander of the Guards Brigade, Brigadier Murray, decided that either the Scots Guards or the Irish Guards would have to be with-drawn and the tanks at his command sent to the help of the troops left on the start line. He made up his mind to send them to the Scots Guards and gave orders for the withdrawal of the two companies of the Irish. But it was after six o'clock in the morning before the order to withdraw was received; for until a wireless set was repaired by a signaller, who risked his life working on it by the light of a shaded torch, the Irish Guards were out of touch with

Left : Fifth Army vehicles move out from Nettuno along the road to Rome.
Above : The Fascist-built settlement known to the Allies as 'the Factory'

Brigade Headquarters. By the time the two companies came back, screened by billows of drifting smoke provided by the artillery, they had suffered further heavy casualties.

Now the attack towards the start line had to be mounted again; and this time by daylight. The third company of the Irish Guards was sent forward, with a company of the 1st King's Shropshire Light Infantry, supported by tanks of the 46th Royal Tank Regiment and the American 894th Tank Destroyer Battalion. On this occasion the attack was successful. The Germans, tired and weakened by their night defence and the battering which the Guards had given them, withdrew towards Campoleone.

By three o'clock in the afternoon the start line was secure and two battalions of the British 3rd Brigade, the 1st Duke of Wellington's Regiment and the 1st King's Shropshire Light Infantry, were ready to advance towards Campoleone. Neither of them reached it that day. By nightfall the men of the King's Shropshire Light Infantry, who had managed to take a hundred prisoners on the way, were established on a ridge overlooking Campoleone station; the Duke of Wellington's Regiment, which had had stronger opposition to overcome, were digging in south of the bridge that carried the railroad tracks over the road leading from Anzio up to Route 7. Another night was to pass before the advance could be resumed.

On the right the Americans had been no more successful. The attack in this sector had been led by seven hundred of Colonel Darby's specially trained and selected troops, the Rangers, experts in night attacks and street fighting. Their task had been to creep through the American lines in the darkness, to break into Cisterna, clear the

Germans out of it, and turn it into a powerful stronghold behind the enemy front, a stronghold from which invaluable support could be given to the advance of General Truscott's 3rd Division.

The Rangers were to crawl forward by way of the Fossa di Pantano, a narrow ditch that extended from the Mussolini Canal to within two miles of Cisterna on the Nettuno-Cisterna road. They were waiting to do so on the 28th when the company commanders of the Grenadier Guards, on their way to the conference that never took place, were killed in their jeep. The consequent delay had given the Germans time to increase their strength in the Cisterna area. The Hermann Göring Division, which had been rather thinly holding the line in front of Cisterna, was reinforced on the night of the 28th by men, tanks and guns from the 26th Panzer Grenadiers, and elements of the 715th Division. By the time the attack could take place on the night of the 30th, Cisterna and its environs were strongly defended by large numbers of well armed German troops.

Unaware of this, the Rangers crept forward through the narrow, muddy ditch, carrying as many hand grenades as they could fit into their pockets, with two bandoleers across their shoulders, but otherwise lightly equipped, except for bazookas and wireless sets. It was a very cold, dark night of low cloud. The Rangers moved forward silently, halting motionless at the sound of enemy movement overhead. And it seemed, when the men leading the long, straggling column in the ditch debouched on to the Cisterna road behind the German front, that they had come through undetected.

In fact, long before the first Rangers in the column emerged from the Fossa de Pantano, their advance had been observed. Instructed to hold their fire until certain of causing the severest casualties, the Germans waited until more and more of the Americans came out of the ditch and went forward towards the waiting rifles, tanks and guns in the houses of Cisterna.

When the column had approached to within five hundred yards of the town, the German fire began. It was intensive, accurate and mercilessly destructive. One of the battalion commanders was killed almost at once, the other was seriously wounded; many of their officers became casualties within minutes, the rest took their men away in small groups to fight back from what cover they could find. By dawn the next day, only a few survivors were holding out in a group of houses and irrigation ditches outside Cisterna. They were surrounded by Germans, and could not hope to hold out much longer. The Germans advanced towards them, using American prisoners as hostages, threatening to shoot the prisoners unless they all surrendered, shouting 'Come out or your comrades die.' Most of them did come out, but far more could not for they were dead or wounded. In a desperate bid to rescue his two battalions, Colonel Darby sent his third battalion down the road, supported by tanks and self-propelled guns. But for all the determination and courage of the Rangers' frontal assault, there could be no saving the beleaguered remnants of their 1st and 3rd Battalions now. Of the 767 Rangers who had crawled forward through the Fossa de Pantano in the early hours of the morning, only six eventually returned. Nor were the men of the 3rd Division, though they fought determindedly all that day to reach Cisterna, able to break through the seemingly impregnable German defences. Continually their officers called for support from tanks and tank destroyers, but the vehicles could not get across the irrigation ditches that criss-crossed the flat, open farmland. By evening, American casualties had risen so high that the attack had to be called off.

So the Americans had failed at Cisterna, just as the British had failed at Campoleone. And nor were these

German troops killed in the battles for 'the Factory'

Engineers neutralize explosives in Anzio

the only two bitter disappointments that General Lucas had to face. For his hopes that the American tanks of General Harmon's 1st Armoured Division would be able to swing round to the left of the British positions and up towards the Alban Hills were also unfulfilled.

The country through which the 1st Division were to move seemed from a study of aerial photographs to be almost ideal tank country, open and free of obstacles, the kind of country that tank commanders in Italy had rarely been able to find.

On 29th January the 1st Armoured Division started to move towards this tempting country. The selected start-line was the disused railroad to the left of the bridge at Carroceto where the Bren-gun carriers of the Grenadier Guards patrol had been fired at from 'The Factory' four days before. The tanks drove up to this start-line by way of a farm track to the left of the Anzio-Carroceto road. The track wound its way towards the railroad, past the little streams that branch off from the Moletta, and up across the slightly higher ground of Buonriposo Ridge.

At first all went well. The American tanks and half-tracks rumbled up the track for about two miles. But as soon as they moved off the track and began to fan out towards the start-line they were in difficulties. For not only was the ground soft and sticky and water-logged, but the little streams and ditches that meandered through the valleys were far more formidable ob-stacles than they had appeared to be from the aerial photographs. They were much deeper than had been sup-posed, with banks, covered by tangles of undergrowth and brambles that in places reached a height of twenty or even thirty feet. Tanks could not possibly operate effectively in country-side like this.

During the night of 29th January

many of the vehicles of the Division sank deep into the ground and had to be winched out. And on the 30th after crossing the start-line they fared no better. The leading tanks had advanced little more than a quarter of a mile when they found it impossible to con-tinue. The whole attack had to be called off; the vehicles had to be with-drawn on to the now congested roads and wait behind the lines until the infantry succeeded in opening up a way for them through Campoleone.

This task naturally fell to the British

German prisoners taken during one of the few periods when the battle was going favourably for the attackers

3rd Brigade, two of whose battalions, the King's Shropshire Light Infantry and the Duke of Wellington's, were still on the ridges overlooking Campoleone station to which their attack of 30th January had taken them. The third battalion in the Brigade, the 2nd Sherwood Foresters, was to lead the attack, passing through the positions of the King's Shropshire Light Infantry and down into Campoleone. The attack went in on the morning of 31st January.

The Foresters went past the scattered dug-outs of the King's Shropshire Light Infantry and down the ridge towards the railroad track under a fearful fire. They succeeded in reaching the track; but there they were trapped in a cross-fire so deadly that no troops in the world could get across unaided. Some tanks of the American 1st Division came forward to help them, but the fire of the German guns was so intense and the tanks were so vulnerable as they rumbled along the embankment that their brave effort was bound to fail. Then the leading platoons of the Foresters were

Units of the powerful and cleverly disposed German reinforcements rumble into position

brought back from the line of the railroad so that the Allied artillery could
blast the German defences before the
rest of the battalion made a renewed
attack.

Once again the Foresters attacked,
and once again they were held by the
ferocity of the German fire. Casualties
mounted at an alarming rate; the commanding officer and all his company
commanders were amongst them. In
one company there were no officers left
at all. General Harmon came up in a
tank to see what was holding the British
up, and how soon his tanks could go
through. He soon saw how desperate
the situation was. 'There were dead
bodies everywhere,' he said afterwards. 'I have never seen so many dead
men in one place. They lay so close I
had to step with care. I shouted for
the commanding officer.

'From a fox-hole there arose a mud-
covered corporal with a handle-bar
moustache. He was the highest-ranking
officer still alive. He stood stiffly to
attention.

"How is it going?" I asked. The
answer was all around me.

"Well, sir," the Corporal said, "there
were a hundred and sixteen of us when
we first came up, and there are sixteen
of us left."

In the whole of the battalion at the
end of the day there were eight officers
left and less than a hundred and fifty
men. The Sherwood Foresters had all
but been destroyed.

The bid for Campoleone had finally
failed. There could be no question now
of General Harmon's tanks getting
through on to the road to Albano. There
could be no question either of General
Truscott's men getting through to
Cisterna.

The order was given for the 1st Armoured Division to pull back to the Padiglione Woods. There seemed nothing for
it but to recognise that the beachhead
was now a defensive line. The Fifth
Army had not been on the defensive
since Salerno.

The Germans counterattack

'It must be driven home to the enemy that the fighting power of Germany is unbroken and that the invasion is an undertaking that will be crushed in the blood of British soldiers.' The Führer's Order of the Day read out to the men of the German Fourteenth Army in the first week of February 1944.

'I had hoped that we were hurling a wild cat on to the shore, but all we had got was a stranded whale.' Churchill's exasperated comment well reflected the feeling of gloom and frustration that overcame the Allied commanders in Italy at the beginning of February 1944.

General Lucas, who feared that, although he had done his best, his 'head would probably fall into the basket', wrote of General Clark's 'gloomy attitude'. Clark himself, with his Army divided and neither part, as Lucas put it, 'capable of inflicting a real defeat on the hostile troops facing it', blamed the Corps commander for not being more aggressive on D-Day, although loyal as always to his subordinates, he defended Lucas to Alexander. The Divisional commanders also were painfully aware how Lucas's caution in the early days of the operation, his 'almost obsessional' fear of being pushed off the beaches by a strong German counterattack, had now landed them in the perilous situation in which they found themselves. Generals Truscott and Penney, in particular, had cause to feel anxious for their divisions which by advancing towards Cisterna and Campoleone had created bulges in the beachhead for whose defences they were now responsible. At least Truscott could comfort himself that the Pontine Marshes, stretching away beyond the Mussolini Canal on his right flank, afforded him protection on that side. For General Penney, however, there were no such

General Eberhard von Mackensen, placed in charge of the German forces at Anzio, plots his manoeuvres

natural defences. His Division was pushed out into the German defences along the Anzio-Albano road like a sore finger, as some of his officers put it, 'dangerously exposed and sensitive on every side'. Yet Penney could obtain no instructions from Corps Headquarters that would allow him to pull it back.

Indeed, it was difficult to get a firm and unequivocal decision from Corps Headquarters about anything. The war correspondents who went there for their occasional briefings came away as confused as they had been when they arrived.

The correspondents sought enlightenment from General Lucas about what was to happen next. 'He received them in his small villa at Nettuno,' wrote one of them. 'He sat in his chair before the fire, and the light shone on his polished cavalry boots. He had the round face and the greying moustaches of a kindly country solicitor. His voice was low and hardly reached the outer circle of the waiting Press men.

'They fired their questions at him, above all Question No. 1, "What was our plan on landing and what had happened to it now?"

'The General looked thoughtful. "Well gentlemen, there was some suggestion that we should aim at getting to those hills" — he turned to his G-2 [Colonel Langevin] — "What's the name of them, Joe?"

'"But the enemy was now strong, far stronger than we had thought."' There was a long pause, and the firelight played on the waiting audience and flickered up to the dark ceiling. Then the General added quickly, "I'll tell you what, gentlemen. That German is a mighty tough fighter. Yes, a mighty tough fighter."

'With that official statement we had, for the moment, to be content.'

All that was certain at the beginning of that first week of February was that the weather, clear and bright on the 1st and 2nd of the month, had broken; that Allied casualties

German machine gun position

already amounted to nearly 6,500 men; that German shelling had increased in intensity; and that, with low clouds and rain driving across the narrow beachhead and the Allied air forces grounded, the long-expected German counterattack would soon be launched.

VI Corps was now engaged in a 'hell of a struggle', Lucas mournfully recorded. 'The situation is crowded with doubt and uncertainty. I expect to be counterattacked in some force, maybe considerable force.'

When General Alexander came over to the beachhead on 1st February, Lucas found him 'kind enough', but it was clear that he was 'not pleased'. 'There were just too many Germans here for me to lick and they could build up faster than I could,' Lucas continued in his diary. 'As I told Clark yesterday, I was sent on a desperate mission, one where the odds were

greatly against success, and I went without saying anything because I was given an order and my opinion was not asked.'

At least Lucas had cause to congratulate himself on the efficient way in which the port was operating, but when he told Alexander that he could support another two divisions in the beachhead, all he got in reply was a mysterious smile. 'He is not easy to talk to,' Lucas decided, 'as he really knows very little of tactics as Americans understand it and I still have trouble because I don't understand the British very well.'

His relationship with General Clark was different. Clark harassed him and prodded him; but at least he liked his American superior and was comforted to know that he supported him against the British.

'Within the next few days the "Battle for Rome" will begin,' the Führer told his armies, encouraging them to ensure that this counterattack would lance

'the abscess south of Rome'. 'This battle has a special significance because the landing at Anzio marks the beginning of the invasion of Europe planned for 1944. Strong German forces are to be tied down in areas as far as possible from the bases in Britain where the majority of the invasion troops are still stationed. The object of the Allies is to gain experience for future operations.

'Every soldier must, therefore, be aware of the importance of the battle which the Fourteenth Army has to fight.

'It must be fought with bitter hatred against an enemy who wages a ruthless war of annihilation against the German people and who, without any higher ethical aims, strives for the destruction of Germany and European culture.

As in the battle of Sicily, on the Rapido river, and at Ortona it must be driven home to the enemy that the fighting power of Germany is unbroken and that the invasion of the year 1944 is an undertaking that will be crushed in the blood of British soldiers.'

By the time Kesselring received this emotional injunction he was more confident than he had been since the day of the Allied invasion. Already he had told General Eberhard von Mackensen, commander of the Fourteenth Army, who had now taken over command of the German forces at Anzio, 'I regard our position of defence as consolidated and we no longer have to reckon with any major reverses'. Kesselring had given him two tasks: to strengthen the defence ring, and to initiate measures to narrow and remove the bridgehead.

By the beginning of February the opportunity for which Kesselring and Mackensen had been waiting had come. The Allies' navies were too busy supplying the Anzio beachhead for them to consider another landing elsewhere, and the bad weather seriously hampered their air operations. The attacks which the American Fifth Army were making on the Gustav Line were being held; and since the British Eighth Army had been forced to thin its ranks in order to reinforce the Cassino front, German troops could with impunity be taken from the Adriatic coastline. The Germans, like the Allies, had suffered heavy casualties in the fighting at Anzio so far. In addition to losing 5,500 men killed and wounded, they had lost nearly fifteen hundred prisoners. During the recent fighting they had been slightly outnumbered by the Allies, and, although the Allied command did not suspect it at the time, they had on occasions been close to falling back before the weight and determination of the British and American attacks.

But German reinforcements continued to arrive at Anzio. They arrived piecemeal so that the line was in a constantly fluid state with an unending succession of arrivals, departures, groupings, regroupings, mergings and partitionings'; yet Mackensen disposed

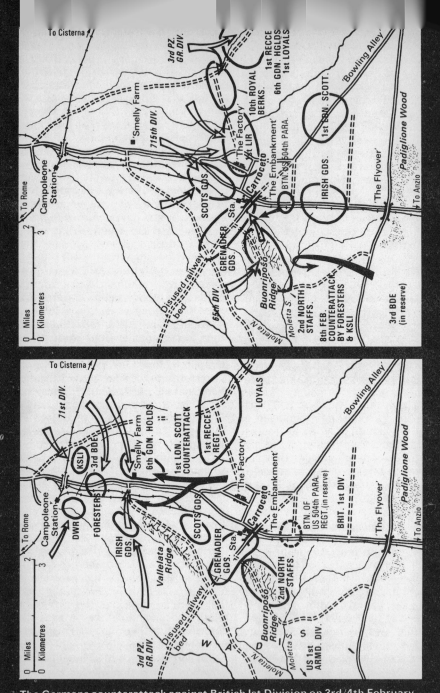

The Germans counterattack against British 1st Division on 3rd/4th February (left) and again from 7th to 10th February

them well, and his front, while constantly in flux, was always strong.

His forces were organised at the beginning of February into two corps. I Parachute Corps with the 4th Parachute Division and the 65th Infantry Division under command, held the front from Albano to the coast by the mouth of the Moletta; the 76th Panzer Corps, with units from five different divisions, held the other half of the line from Albano to the coast by the Mussolini Canal. The 3rd Panzer Grenadiers were astride the vital Albano Road. The 26th Panzer Grenadier Division was in reserve.

At first Kesselring had considered attacking the beachhead from the north, but for fear of his troops coming under bombardment from the Allied fleets he dropped this plan and concentrated his attention on the Albano-Anzio road, on the long bulge, three miles long and one-and-a-half miles wide, pointing towards Campoleone which the British 1st Division were protecting with understandable apprehension. A successful advance down this road to the sea would cut the beachhead in half and allow the German troops to destroy the Allies piece by piece. To reach the road it would be necessary to pierce and slice through the salient in the British sector, and plans were developed with this object in mind.

The salient, which Mackensen's Chief of Staff described as 'positively demanding' attack, was far less strongly defended than General Penney would have liked. At the top of it, still looking across towards Campoleone station and the Cisterna to Rome railroad tracks, was the 3rd Brigade, the Duke of Wellington's Regiment to the left of the Anzio road, the King's Shropshire Light Infantry to the right of it. The sadly depleted Sherwood Foresters were farther back astride the road itself.

Behind the Duke of Wellington's Regiment was the Guards Brigade, facing the difficult gully-riven countryside beyond the Vallelata Ridge at the head of the Moletta where General Harmon's tanks had bogged down at the end of January. This countryside was now known as the 'wadi' country because of the gullies' resemblance to the dry, rocky watercourses with which the troops had grown familiar in North Africa. Immediately south of the Duke of Wellington's, in front of the Sherwood Foresters, were the Irish Guards. South again of the Irish Guards were the Scots Guards; and south of them were the Grenadier Guards defending the immediate area of 'The Factory' at Carroceto. Along the eastern edge of the bulging salient, south of the King's Shropshire Light Infantry, occupying an area generally known as 'Smelly Farm', were the 6th Gordon Highlanders. South of them patrolling the woodland area northeast of 'The Factory' were the 1st Reconnaissance Regiment. South of the Reconnaissance Regiment, at the base of the salient on the east, were the 1st Loyals. Behind them, on the other side of the base of the salient facing west, were the 2nd North Staffordshire Regiment. Most of these battalions, and in particular the 6th Gordons and the Irish Guards which were dug in on shallow-ridges on either side of the Anzio-Albano road, were dangerously over-extended.

They were also dangerously placed. The 'wadi' country to the west and the woodland to the east provided good cover for the Germans to move about unseen by day and to form up for fighting patrols and probing attacks by night.

Several of these probing attacks were made during the first days of February on the 3rd Brigade which had little need now of the Division's warning that 'strong counterattacks' were to be expected. Indeed, there was not a unit in the whole of the Divisional area that needed the warning. Both the King's Shropshire Light Infantry and the Duke of Wellington's Regiment had been harried by fighting patrols that had crept by night across the railroad tracks; the Guards

Brigade, the North Staffordshires, the Gordon Highlanders and the Loyals had all been attacked. The Reconnaissance Regiment reported greatly increased tank activity in the woodland to the east; from the west, on the afternoon of the 3rd, an enormous flock of sheep came running over the Vallelata Ridge towards the positions of the Irish Guards, driven, it was supposed, by the Germans who wanted to test the ground in front of them for mines.

Mines, as it happened, were in short supply; so, too, was wire. Nor could General Penney console himself with the thought that, when attacked, he would be well supported by tanks. The Divisional tanks were concentrated in the area of 'The Factory'; but the far more numerous tanks of General Harmon's 1st Armoured Division were almost five miles away to the rear in the Padiglione Woods. Penney knew that his Divisional artillery was reliable; but its effectiveness could not be guaranteed once the enemy had infiltrated large bodies of troops through the gaps in the Division's defences and there was no longer a known front line.

As twilight fell on the evening of 3rd February, the rain grew heavier and the men of the 1st Division prepared themselves for another unpleasant night. At first the night seemed quieter than usual; the darkness was occasionally and violently lit by a bursting shell, an exploding mortar bomb, or a stream of tracer bullets flying overhead. But there were no other indications that the dreaded German counterattack was about to begin. Then, just after eleven o'clock, the head of the salient occupied by the three battalions of the 3rd Brigade came under sudden and ferocious artillery fire. The artillery barrage then moved down the western side of the salient to ravage the positions of the Irish Guards.

As soon as the barrage lifted German infantry of the 3rd Panzer Grenadiers, together with strong supporting units, launched their attack. Indeed, the attack had already begun, unknown to the Guards, some time before; for several companies of Panzer Grenadiers had infiltrated the Brigade position. And as waves of troops surged over the ridges from the 'wadi' country, shouting 'Sieg Heil! Sieg Heil! Got mit uns!' as a previous generation of Germans had done in the mud of Flanders, the Guardsmen found themselves under simultaneous attack from the rear.

The Irish Guards were greatly outnumbered, but they were not immediately overwhelmed. Their steady, accurate fire tore holes in the enemy ranks. But the Germans fought with the determination and courage that the Führer had demanded; and to the Guardsmen it seemed that there was no end to the numbers of them closing in on every side.

While the Guardsmen struggled to hold the enemy off, the Gordon Highlanders, on the opposite side of the salient, came under as sudden and fierce attack from the reinforced 71st Infantry Division. The Germans forced their way between two of the Gordons' companies, one of which retired without orders, and then pushed on fast towards the main road north of 'The Factory'. Soon afterwards German tanks, too, had cut through the Gordons' position and were firing up and down the main road. Across the road the 3rd Panzer Grenadiers and the 71st Infantry Division linked forces behind the Sherwood Foresters.

The Germans' first objective had been achieved: the British 3rd Brigade, and with it the top of the salient, had been successfully cut off, the area occupied by the Gordons to the east of the Albano Road had been largely overrun. It was 10.00 hours on 4th February.

It was raining harder than ever, so that there was no hope of help for the British Division from Allied aircraft. Nor was there any hope for the Division from General Harmon's tanks; for, although General Lucas had lacon-

Battleweary paratroops keep the Allies cooped up in their beachead

ically ordered General Penney, 'You'd better get your boys out of it', he felt unable to release the 1st Armoured Division to assist Penney in this otherwise difficult, if not impossible, task.

Already Lucas had reinforced Penney's Division with the 3rd Battalion of the American 504th Parachute Regiment, which was held in reserve around Carroceto; but this was not enough for the strong counterattack which would now have to be launched against the Germans before they established themselves firmly on the ground they had won in the night and in the early hours of the morning. As it was, they were hourly consolidating their hold on the Albano road between Campoleone and Carroceto, since the bad weather prevented any air strikes against the forward movements of their reserves, and the Allied artillery could not alone prevent these reserves from reaching the forward German positions. It was essential that Penney counterattack and extricate his 3rd Brigade before nightfall allowed the enemy to gain any further strength in the area.

At this crucial moment there arrived at Anzio a brigade from the British 56th Division which had been fighting at Cassino. It was Brigadier Kenneth Davidson's 168th Infantry Brigade comprising the 10th Royal Berkshires, the 1st London Irish Rifles and the 1st London Scottish.

General Penney urgently asked for the use of this Brigade in extracting his own 3rd Brigade from the head of the salient. Lucas demurred; he would need them as he would need Harmon's 1st Armoured Division for the still heavier German attacks impending. But Penney was insistent, and eventually Lucas gave way.

Immediately Penney gave orders for the London Scottish to launch a counterattack in the 'Smelly Farm' area where the Gordons were holding on so precariously against rapidly in-

creasing German pressure. The infantry attack, supported by the tanks of the 46th Royal Tank Regiment, was to go in at four o'clock that afternoon, while the two other battalions of the 168th Brigade moved forward into close reserve.

The attack began on time. The London Scottish moved up beside the Albano road and into the dangerous area of the 'Smelly Farm'. They moved quickly and well, skilfully taking one unprepared German position after another, capturing and sending back several prisoners. When their successful attack was at length interrupted by heavy artillery fire, orders were issued for the 3rd Brigade to come back as quickly as they could through the corridor which the London Scottish had partially opened up for them.

The Sherwood Foresters and the Duke of Wellington's, in accordance with instructions already given, broke off contact with the enemy and began their withdrawal first, leaving the

'The Factory' receives another artillery onslaught

King's Shropshire Light Infantry to keep the Germans at bay. Under fierce artillery fire and in pouring rain the survivors of the two battalions moved back towards 'The Factory' at Carroceto, carrying those too badly wounded to walk, protected to some extent by the Allied guns that maintained a constant fire around the edges of the salient.

Many tanks, vehicles, guns and a good deal of equipment were left behind, burning in the rain; casualties rose as the artillery fire on the crowded road to Carroceto increased and as groups of Germans in the fields and buildings on either side of it opened fire on the retreating troops with machine-guns and mortars. Night brought no safety, for the sky was bright with flames from burning hayricks and vehicles and from the Verey lights continually falling through the smoke.

Fourteen-hundred men did not return; over nine-hundred of these, so the Germans claimed, had been taken prisoner. The Germans had constantly called out in English, 'It's hopeless. You'd better join us'. And many had done so. But the Germans had suffered nearly as heavily as the British; and the 3rd Brigade survived. The withdrawal, an unpleasant and difficult operation in any circumstances, had been carried out with great skill. The salient had been cut back; yet the line still held.

No one could doubt, however, that it would not be long before the Germans renewed their attack on the beachhead and endeavoured to follow up their initial success by renewing their advance. It seemed more than likely that this advance would be continued along the axis of the Albano-Anzio road. At Corps Headquarters, the Intelligence staff received an almost continual stream of reports giving information of the arrival or pending arrival of more and more German units in the Anzio area.

Above: British and American prisoners under the shadow of the Coliseum while Rome was still in German hands. *Above right:* German paratrooper captures a few moments peace in the Nettuno countryside

While Mackensen deployed these units, Mark Clark arrived once again at the beachhead. He was more than ever disturbed by the situation he discovered, particularly by the shortage of ammunition and by the reduced strength of the British 1st Division. More reinforcements had been landed at Anzio over the past few days; but there were never enough of them to fill up the depleted ranks at the front.

Clark consequently gave orders for the construction of a final beachhead defence behind the existing front on a line following that which the Allies had held on the third day of the operation. The Allies worked with an almost frantic haste to get this line completed before the Germans attacked again. The line extended from the mouth of the Moletta, across 'The Flyover' bridge from which the Grenadier Guards had set out on their first patrol on 24th January, towards Padiglione and down to the Mussolini Canal. Protected by minefields and coils of barbed wire, this line was intended to form a barrier beyond which there could be no retreat. Behind it every available gun was concentrated to give its defenders support. The enemy 'thinks he can drive me back into the ocean', Lucas recorded in his diary. 'Maybe so, but it will cost him.'

On the right of the line by the Mussolini Canal were the First Special Service Force, a well-trained unit of 1,800 Americans and Canadians, which had arrived at Anzio on 2nd February. On the far left was a regiment of the 45th American Division. The 3rd American Division still faced Cisterna; and the 1st British Division was still in the centre west of the Anzio-Albano road, supported by the 509th Parachute Battalion and part of the 504th

Parachute Regiment. In reserve in the Padiglione Woods was the American 1st Armoured Division, and two regiments of the 45th Division.

In the centre, the 1st Division did all it could to ensure that the existing front held firm under the next German onslaught. General Penney, making the best use he could of the tired and weakened battalions at his disposal, gave the recently arrived and relatively fresh 168th Brigade the vital task of defending the area of 'The Factory'. The 1st London Irish were placed inside the battered buildings themselves, the 10th Royal Berkshires were ordered to occupy and hold the ground to their right, the 1st London Scottish, who had done so well on the afternoon and evening of 4th February, were held in reserve south west of Carroceto. Responsible for the defence of Carroceto were two battalions of the Guards Brigade – the Scots Guards and the Grenadiers – the Scots Guards stretched northwards from Carroceto along the railroad track towards Cam-

poleone, the Grenadiers holding a line north westwards from Carroceto along 'The Embankment' – known to the Americans as 'The Bowling Alley' – that carried the disused railroad towards the 'wadi' country. The third Guards battalion, the Irish Guards, together with their American friends of the 3rd Battalion of the 504th Parachute Regiment, were in reserve, to the left of the London Scottish, behind Carroceto village. To the left of them, on the Buonriposo Ridge, were the 2nd North Staffordshires. The two other battalions in the 2nd Brigade, the 1st Loyals and the 6th Gordon Highlanders, were with the Reconnaissance Regiment on the other flank, facing east towards the woodlands north of Padiglione. The 3rd Brigade which had had so gruelling a time in the past few days was pulled back for a rest.

Not that there could be a proper rest even for them. The enemy shelling had died down in its intensity, but it never died out altogether, and 'Anzio Annie' persistently continued to rumble out of her tunnel to lob shells high over the front.

For the troops along 'The Embankment' and around 'The Factory' there could scarcely be any rest at all; and General Penney, knowing how imminent the German attack must be, could not allow them the least lapse from vigilance. The pilots of Allied aircraft, getting off the ground on one of the rare flying days in the first week of the month, reported that more and more German guns appeared to be concentrating north of Campoleone. Intelligence reports indicated that these guns would open up in a barrage heralding a German attack on the night of 7th February. Growing numbers of deserters from the German lines confirmed that this was probably the chosen date.

Mackensen had firmly decided that this attack must be made once more down the Albano-Anzio road through Carroceto. It was to be another pincer attack; the 65th Infantry Division would go in from the west, the 3rd Panzer Grenadier Division would attack from the east, driving the enemy from 'The Factory' area, and then turning south for Anzio and Nettuno.

While preparing for this attack on the British, Mackensen kept the Americans on their own front by sending in several probing attacks near Cisterna, one of which led to the recapture of Ponte Rotto, a village on the Cisterna-Padiglione road captured at the cost of heavy casualties by General Truscott's Division after the tragic failure of the Rangers' attempted *coup de main*. But these attacks on the Cisterna front did nothing to persuade VI Corps headquarters that the main assault would be directed not against the Americans but against the British, against 'The Factory' and Carroceto – the twin keys to the gate to the sea.

When day dawned on 7th February it was raining hard. It went on raining all morning. The dispirited troops knew that if the Germans were, indeed, to make their attack that day, there could be no hope of support from the Allied air forces. The Germans would be able to form up undisturbed in the 'wadi' country beyond the Buonriposo Ridge to the west and in the woods to the east of 'The Factory'. It continued to rain all day. As darkness gathered again an unnatural quiet fell over the sodden fields.

And then, at about eleven o'clock at night, the silence was broken all over the 1st Division's front – and behind it. For the Germans, as in their past attacks, had infiltrated through the gaps in the front under cover of darkness, had set up machine-gun posts and strong-points in the rear of the British trenches; and, when the main attack was under way and the Verey lights went up, they opened fire on their enemies from behind.

From the west, the German troops came pouring up Buonriposo Ridge, firing their rifles, throwing grenades, shouting 'Sieg Heil! Sieg Heil! Gott mit uns!' at the North Staffordshires. Within minutes the North Staffordshires, under attack from both front and rear and drawn into a confusing and savage hand-to-hand struggle around their forward trenches, were fighting for their lives. The radio sets of all but one of their companies went off the air; Battalion Headquarters was surrounded; most of their officers were killed or wounded. Within an hour they had been driven off the top of Buonriposo Ridge. As a company of the Irish Guards came up from the main road to help the North Staffordshires, the Germans reformed on the Ridge to turn their attack northeast, to move down upon the Grenadier Guards along 'The Embankment' outside Carroceto.

The rain had stopped and the moon had come up as the Germans poured down on the Grenadier Guards, so dangerously exposed by the defeat of the North Staffordshires. There were a lot of them, a Grenadiers officer commented, and they appeared to have 'suddenly materialized, as it seemed, out of the air'. Soon the Grenadiers were involved in as savage and confusing a fight as the North Staffordshires had been. Split up into small, unco-ordinated groups by the strength and suddenness of the German attack, they struggled, sometimes successfully, sometimes not, to hold their ground. As one group, larger than others, tried to withdraw to a farmhouse on the outskirts of Carroceto in order to rally and bring more coherence into the defence, the Americans of the 504th Parachute Regiment hurried up the road to Carroceto to do what they could to stem the German tide.

No sooner had the Americans arrived and taken up a defensive position south of 'The Embankment' close to the Battalion Headquarters of the Grenadier Guards than this Headquarters came under fierce attack. It was situated in the Fossa di Carroceto, a deep gully which began near 'The Embankment' and stretched back southwards between the main road and Buonriposo Ridge. The bottom of the gully was covered with a tangle of brambles concealing a ditch over which there was but a single crossing-place. This crossing-place was guarded by the Grenadiers' Headquarters Support Company, commanded by Major the Hon WP Sidney. As the Germans rushed down towards this crossing-place and threatened to break through on to the main road south of Carroceto, Major Sidney ran towards them firing his tommy-gun. When the gun jammed he hurled a succession of grenades across the ditch. Two Guardsmen crept forward to help him; one of them was killed when a grenade was detonated prematurely and Sidney himself was wounded in the legs. But he kept throwing grenades which the survivor of his two supporters primed for him. As other men in his company managed to scramble forward to the threatened crossing-place to aid him he was wounded again when fragments of a stick-grenade hit him in the face. By

German soldier hurls a stick grenade from his well made trench position

then the German attack had faltered, and Major Sidney (now Lord de l'Isle) had earned the V.C.

The German attack on the Fossa di Carroceto was resumed in the early hours of the morning. Yet again the Grenadiers, well supported by the American paratroops, held firm. By dawn the Grenadiers' strength had been reduced to twenty men, that of the Americans to forty-five. The Germans, however, had for the moment been held. Buonriposo Ridge was in their hands; but they had not yet reached the road. Nor yet had they reached it from the east.

On this side of the 1st Division's front, the positions of the 10th Royal Berks had been infiltrated in the same way as those of the North Stafford-shires on Buonriposo Ridge. The men of the 3rd Panzer Grenadier Division had pushed their way in the darkness between the forward trenches, and through a gap between the Royal Berks and the Reconnaissance Regiment. They had also thrown a platoon of the London Irish Rifles off its ground to the east of 'The Factory'. And then, shortly before midnight, the main attack had been launched upon the Royal Berkshire Regiment guarding the eastern approaches to 'The Factory'. The Reconnaissance Regiment and the Gordon High-landers further south had also come under heavy attack; the Reconnais-sance Regiment had been forced to give ground and a platoon of the Gordons had been overwhelmed. Yet, as the Germans had failed to reach the road in the west, so in this sector they failed to reach the starting-line they had hoped to gain for an assault upon 'The Factory'.

During the night's fighting, however, the Germans had gained one supreme advantage: the high, dominating ground of Buonriposo Ridge. If they were allowed to remain in occupation

Effective German bombing in the streets of Nettuno. Four American and one British vehicle were destroyed

of it, there could be little doubt that they would soon also gain possession of both Carroceto and 'The Factory'.

At dawn on 8th February, General Penney addressed himself to the task of recapturing this vital ground before the enemy tightened their hold upon it. It was an appallingly difficult task, for the only troops he had which could be spared for it were the Sherwood Foresters and the King's Shropshire Light Infantry, two battalions that had suffered so severely in the fighting of 3rd and 4th February. The rest of the Division in addition to being 'dog tired', as the commanding officer of the Royal Berkshires described his men, were still in face of the enemy; they could not possibly be withdrawn.

So General Penney, since he could extract no reinforcements from Corps Headquarters, had no alternative to the use of these two battered, though somewhat reinforced, battalions from the 3rd Brigade. He gave them the support of a squadron from the Reconnaissance Regiment and a squadron of the 46th Royal Tank Regiment. Not that he expected that tanks would be able to do much to support the infantry in the difficult, muddy ground at the foot of Buonriposo Ridge – as, indeed, in the event, they were not.

The counterattack, planned in a mood almost of desperation, failed as it seemed bound to fail. The Sherwood Foresters and the King's Shropshire Light Infantry both fought bravely throughout the afternoon in the cold and pouring rain to reach the summit of the Ridge. The Foresters, who had suffered heavy casualties in an artillery barrage before the attack began, suffered heavier casualties still in the subsequent fighting. The King's Shropshire Light Infantry fell into a trap; all the company commanders were killed or wounded, and the men were brought back to the Fossa di Carroceto by their senior NCOs.

With his last reserves expended, with the obvious danger that troops defending 'The Factory' might not be able to withstand a further assault, General Penney left for Corps Headquarters to try once more to extract some help from General Lucas. But Lucas felt unable to grant him any; he had nothing to spare from Corps reserve, he said. The 1st Division must stay where it was and hold its ground at all costs.

For some time now General Penney had felt that the staff at Corps Headquarters failed utterly to appreciate the problems he had to face out in his cold and isolated salient. His units, it sometimes seemed to him, were no more to the senior officers in the deep cellar at Nettuno than dots on the maps that hung upon the wall. He doubted that General Lucas himself had the confidence and determination to conduct a successful defence of the beachhead.

General Lucas, for his part, appeared to doubt that Penney's Division was up to its job. He was reluctant to send forward precious reserves to prop it up when it was so dangerously unstable. He might lose his reserves and the battle for Anzio with it. 'I wish I had an American Division in there,' wrote Lucas on the evening of 8th February. 'It is probably my fault that I don't understand them better. I think they suffer excessive losses. They are certainly brave men but ours are better trained, in my opinion, and I am sure that our officers are better educated in a military way.'

The tension and distrust on the battlefield was reflected in the atmosphere at the headquarters of the higher command. General Alexander, anxious to obtain some relief for the over-extended and badly mauled British 1st Division at Anzio, had already appealed to Mark Clark to bring some of the worst hit units out of the line to give them a chance to recover. But Clark had been adamant. 'I told him,' he reports in his memoirs, 'that if any of the British 1st Division was to come out of the beachhead now it was over my strongest objection and that he would have to give me an order in writing. He said the British 1st Division was tired. I told him so was the 3rd but that if the situation got more critical all would have to fight whether they were tired or not.'

While Alexander had his differences with Clark, and Penney had his with Lucas, the Prime Minister in London felt a growing sense of disillusionment with the whole operation. It had all been 'a great disappointment' to him. On the day that the Sherwood Foresters and the King's Shropshire Light Infantry made their unsuccessful attempt to retake Buonriposo Ridge, Churchill sent a cable to enquire how many vehicles had been landed at Anzio 'by the seventh and fourteenth days respectively. I should be glad,' he further asked, 'if it were possible without too much trouble or delay, to distinguish trucks, cannon and tanks.'

The reply to this cable came as a shock to him. 12,350 vehicles, including 356 tanks, had been landed by the seventh day; 21,940 vehicles, including 380 tanks, by the fourteenth. This meant that there was one vehicle for every four men.

'Thank you for your information,' Churchill responded. 'How many of our men are driving or looking after 18,000 vehicles in this narrow space? We must have a great superiority of chauffeurs.'

Churchill was particulary disturbed because he had recently received from the United States Chiefs of Staff a message expressing their concern about the Italian campaign. They wanted to know what was being planned and what General Wilson's views on the matter were. Churchill passed on the message to Wilson who admitted that the troops at Anzio had been contained; he blamed the Corps commander – by now a universal scapegoat – who was suffering from a 'Salerno complex'. Lucas had repeatedly been pushed 'from above', but the pressure had had no effect.

Churchill sent a copy of Wilson's reply to Washington with an accompanying message to the effect that even if there were to be a battle of attrition at Anzio, as the American Chiefs of Staff feared there would be, this would surely be 'better than standing by and watching the Russians fight'. And, in any case, the fighting in Italy was successfully drawing German divisions away from other fronts. Yet Churchill had to admit that things were not going as well in Italy as he had hoped. 'All this,' he said, 'has been a disappointment to me.'

While the disgruntled Allied commanders grew more and more anxious, Mackensen prepared his plans for the capture of 'The Factory'. The attack was to be led by General Graser with the 725th and 735th Grenadier Regiments of the 715th Division under his command. It was to be preceded by a heavy concentrated artillery barrage on the ground so steadfastly held by the Royal Berkshire Regiment in the earlier fighting.

Before the barrage opened, Kenneth Davidson, the commander of the 168th Brigade, sent a message to all units under his command assuring them 'how much their gallantry and steadfast courage' was appreciated. 'I hope you will understand,' his message continued, 'just what I, at this time, am feeling about you. I hope in the near future you will be relieved, but first we must all produce that extra effort however tired we may be. Good luck. May God's blessing be on you all.'

The Royal Berkshires made the effort; but they were weak and exhausted, and the Germans too strong for them. Their positions were overrun, their Battalion reduced to its Headquarters, two sections of C company, and a few Bren-gun carrier and mortar personnel – forty men in all.

The way now lay open for General Graser to assault the London Irish Rifles in 'The Factory'. And when the attack came, the London Irish, too, were too weak for the overwhelming impetus of the German attack.

The fall of 'The Factory' inevitably exposed to attack the Scots Guards in the village of Carroceto behind it. They fought desperately to hold it; and for the whole of that day, 9th February,

Clearing up in Nettuno

and for the whole of the following night, they did hold it. But by daylight on the 10th they had been forced back to 'The Embankment' where in the still teeming rain the remnants of the Irish Guards were still hanging on in what their History terms 'a litter of smashed equipment and burnt vehicles, shattered ammunition and derelict tanks'. Supporting the Guards in their waterlogged slit trenches were an assortment of survivors from other battalions, gunners and sappers and American paratroops. But they were all reaching the limits of their endurance; and General Penney could not but fear that they must soon give way and break before the fresh German troops that General Graser was able to bring against them.

Once more Penney appealed to Corps Headquarters for help. 'The 1st Division must get help,' he warned. Otherwise it would soon no longer exist. Yet all that General Lucas felt able to give him were some tanks and the 180th Regimental Combat Team of the American 45th Infantry Division. Penney urgently impressed upon Corps Headquarters the inadequacy of this aid. Nothing now would serve except a full-scale counterattack; it was vain to hope that the Germans could be kept at bay by air attacks, for the appalling weather prevented any aircraft leaving the ground. At last at six o'clock on the morning of the 10th, General Lucas, recognising that the British were now too weak to hold on unaided any longer,

agreed. He would order a counterattack on 'The Factory' by the American 45th Infantry Division; and soon after eleven o'clock he came to the Headquarters of the Guards Brigade to deliver his orders.

General Penney attended the meeting with Brigadiers Murray and Davidson of the Guards and 168th Brigades; also present were General Harmon of the American 1st Armoured Division and, of course, General Eagles of the American 45th Infantry Division which was to make the attack. But the only positive orders which General Lucas gave when Penney had explained the position were delivered to General Eagles. They were contained in seven words: 'Okay, Bill, you give 'em the works'.

A whole day's planning was required before these terse instructions could be made into a coherent plan; and by the time the counterattack went in at half past six of the morning of the 11th February the Germans had so strengthened their positions in and around 'The Factory' that it was impossible to dislodge them. The 1st Battalion of the American 179th Infantry Regiment and the American 191st Tank Battalion made valiant efforts to retake the blackened, ruined buildings from which the British had been thrown; but they were unable to dislodge the defenders.

By 12th February the Allies were forced to admit that all their counterattacks had failed.

Attrition

'This is becoming a war of attrition. Until I am considerably reinforced I can't do much about it.' Major-General John P Lucas. Diary entry for 12th February.

While the Germans, having now gained all their initial objectives, reorganised their forces for the final attack which

would drive the invaders into the sea, the Allied commanders strove hard to bring into the beachhead the fresh troops who alone could save it.

The American 45th Infantry Division had suffered many casualties in their counterattacks on 'The Factory'; the American 3rd Division, hard-pressed along the southeastern perimeter of the beachhead, was becoming increasingly tired; the British 1st Division was now so badly battered that it could no longer be considered a fighting unit.

But where could reinforcements be found? The British were critically short of manpower. Years of full mobilisation had drained the country's resources. The British Adjutant General complained that he was being forced to break up divisions at the rate of one every two months 'in order to use the men as replacements for the other units committed to action'. Even when reinforcements could be found, there remained the acute shortage of LSTs in which to transport them to the beachhead.

One brigade, the 168th, of Major-General Gerald Templer's 56th (London) Division had arrived on 3rd February and within hours of landing had been sent into action. A second brigade of this Division, the 167th, had landed by the 13th and the third was due to arrive a few days later. These men of the 56th Division were not, however, fresh troops; they had been fighting on the southern front for months, and were due for a rest. But there was no other suitable unit available. And even they had not been sent to Anzio without considerable apprehension. For the southern front was due to flare up again.

On 15th February the monastery at Cassino was bombarded and partially destroyed by Allied aircraft, a day earlier than intended so that the bombers would be available that much sooner to give help to the threatened troops in the Anzio beachhead. The excuse for the bombing was that the monastery was being used as a fortress, although the Germans claimed that there were no troops within four hundred yards of it. In any case, the bombing helped the Germans rather than the Allies; for after the last of the 350 tons of high explosive and incen-

Monte Cassino, where the rest of the 15th Allied Army Group was held up and prevented from joining with the Anzio beachhead until late May

diary bombs had fallen, the Germans moved forward to occupy the ruins in force. The subsequent land battle, conducted by the Allies with insufficient forces, resulted in a further setback for their hopes. On 18th February, General Alexander decided that he had no alternative to breaking it off. By then the battle for Anzio beachhead had already begun.

The Germans had faced the battle for the beachhead with great confidence. They had ample supplies of stores and ammunition; they even had strong support from the Luftwaffe which was a rare pleasure for the German soldier in Italy. Reserves of troops which had continued to arrive ever since the beginning of the month had now built up Mackensen's command into a truly formidable force. The headquarters of the 76th Panzer Corps had arrived from the Adriatic, the 715th (Motorized) Infantry Division from the south of France, the 114th Jäger Division from Yugoslavia. By 15th February there had arrived from the Garigliano the rest of the 29th Panzer Grenadier Division, one of whose battalions had been in the Anzio area at the time of the landing, and, from Doberitz, on Hitler's special orders, three battalions of the Berlin-Spandau Lehr Regiment, a Regiment of dedicated Nazis which the Führer 'valued particularly highly'. By 16th February there had also arrived from Germany a battle group of the 16th SS Panzer Grenadier Division, two battalions of the 1027th Panzer Grenadier Regiment and two battalions of the 1028th Panzer Grenadier Regiment. Although some of these units were under strength, there were, when the last of them arrived on 16th February, the equivalent of six divisions ranged round the beachhead.

'I was convinced,' wrote Kesselring later, 'even taking their powerful naval guns and overwhelming air superiority into consideration, that with the means available we must succeed in throwing the Allies back into the sea. I constantly kept in mind the psychological effects

Above : Major-General John W O'Daniel, 'Iron Mike', commander of 3rd Infantry Division. *Right :* Major-General Gerald Templer, who took over command of the British 1st Division from General Penney

of their situation on the staff and troops of the American VI Corps. Penned in as they were on the low-lying, notoriously unhealthy coast, it must have been damned unpleasant.'

Unpleasant, indeed, it was. It was almost impossible not to suffer from a sense of claustrophobia in that constricted beachhead surrounded by German troops threatening always to close in, throwing shells, as if with impunity, over the Allied lines.

Inside the beachhead the constriction was appalling. There was no space for the echelons which should have been far in the rear to move more than a few miles back from the front. There was nowhere that was safe from shelling; even the Casualty Clearing Stations and the Hospitals were constantly under attack, for the most scrupulous German gunner could scarcely avoid hitting them when they lay so close to his legitimate targets. The American hospital area became known as 'Hell's Half Acre'; and General Harmon said

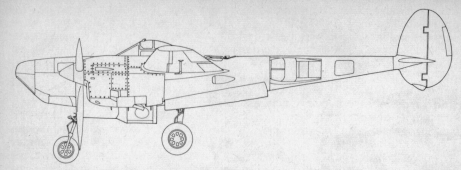

The Lockheed P-38 Lightning was one of the war's most controversial fighters. It was loved by some pilots for its heavy firepower, solid construction, speed in a dive and the security afforded by two engines, and detested by others for its weight, lack of manoeuvrability and slow rate of climb. But one advantage afforded by its twin boom layout was that it was possible to convert the nose to accomodate a bomb aimer to lead other aircraft, or reconnaissance equipment. The P-38L was powered by two Allison V-1710 inlines, 1,475 hp each at take off, had a top speed of 414 mph at 25,000 feet, climbed to 20,000 feet in 7 minutes, had a ceiling of 44,000 feet and a maximum range of 2,600 miles. It weighed 12,800 pounds empty and 21,600 pounds maximum. Span was 52 feet and length 37 feet 10 inches. Basic armament was four .5-inch machine guns and one 20mm cannon (not fitted on reconnaissance and bomb aimer aircraft) and various combinations of rockets and bombs

that some men of the 1st Armoured Division actually declined to report their wounds for fear that they would be taken to it and be killed there.

The 1st Armoured Division were now in reserve once more together with the 1st British Division. Between them the American 45th Division and the 56th (London) Division held most of the front. The 56th faced the 'wadi' country, down from Buonriposo Ridge towards the sea at the mouth of the Moletta; the 45th held the line from Padiglione to the Anzio-Albano road. The 157th Regimental Combat Team, commanded by Colonel John H Church, was responsible for the defence of the road itself and for linking the American defences to the right-hand of the British south of the Buonriposo Ridge. In the centre, facing 'The Factory' was the 179th Regimental Combat Team and, on the right, the 180th. The 3rd Division and the Special Services Force covered the rest of the right flank from the Cisterna-Campomorto road to the sea along the Mussolini Canal.

It was against this part of the front that the mass of the German armour appeared to be assembling. But it was never for a moment supposed that this was other than a feint, that the full force of the attack would not come, as the previous attack had come, down the axis of the Anzio-Albano road. The advantages presented by this approach were obvious: tanks could concentrate in the area around the captured 'Factory', and could manoeuvre in the fields to the east of the road, even if they could not pass through the 'wadi' country to the rest of it. The countryside to the west of the road up to 'The Flyover' and on both sides of the road south of it, where the woodland began, was ideal for the favoured German tactics of infiltration.

On surveying this approach neither Mackensen nor Kesselring had any reservations about the aptness of a frontal assault. Even if the guns of the Allied navies had not made a flank attack too risky to contemplate, the advantages of an attack straight down from 'The Factory' to the sea might well have outweighed any other possible approach. The objective of splitting the enemy force into two and then destroying it piecemeal – an operation often favoured and practised by Napoleon – seemed to the German commanders now well within their grasp since their starting point, 'The Factory', was less than ten miles from Anzio harbour.

Mackensen's plan was simple. It involved throwing the whole weight of the reinforced Fourteenth Army at the Allied centre by night. Part of the 65th Infantry Division and of the 4th Parachute Division were to advance through the 'wadi' country to the west of the main road. At the same time the 715th Infantry Division, the 114th Light Infantry Division, the 3rd Panzer Grenadier Division and various units of the Hermann Göring Division were to attack on a wider front to the east of it. Once the infantry had gone through, the 26th and 29th Panzer Grenadiers, with two battalions of the new Mark V Panther and Mark VI Tiger tanks, would quickly follow them. Germany's latest secret weapon, 'The Goliath', would be used for the first time. 'The Goliath' was a miniature tank about two feet high, self-propelled and remote-controlled. It was filled with explosive which could be detonated by means of a wire, two thousand feet long, when the tank reached its objective.

When Mackensen's proposed plan reached Germany, Hitler had no objection to the use of this, the latest of his secret weapons – in most, if not all, of which he had unbounded faith. But he did object to the attack being carried out on so wide a front. He ordered it to be narrowed into a savage, concentrated, ruthlessly powerful thrust against what he had termed 'the abscess' on the Italian coast. And he ordered this thrust to be led by the Lehr Regiment of selected Nazis, although they had never been in battle before, being used in Germany as demonstration troops on field exercises.

Kesselring and Mackensen accepted this variation to the original plan with reluctance. The Lehr Regiment, recently arrived from Germany, were given no time for that careful reconnaissance of the ground which must precede a night assault. The attack, therefore, would have to be postponed until dawn; and the infiltration tactics which had previously proved so effective would have to be discarded. But, all the same, Kesselring felt confident. He now had over 125,000 troops under his command, a quarter as many again as his opponents. Mackensen did not share his superior's confidence. A more cautious, pessimistic man, he felt uneasy about Hitler's amendment of the original plan since it forced so many troops into so narrow a space; he suggested a delay of one or two days to allow more artillery ammunition to be collected and to give the troops newly arrived from Germany more time to familiarise themselves with the ground. Kesselring refused to consider a delay; and Mackensen asked to be removed to another command – for the third time since his arrival at the beachhead. The request was rejected; the attack must go in as planned.

The German attack was heralded, on 16th February at six o'clock of a damp and foggy morning, by a devastating artillery bombardment, not the creeping barrage, 'reminiscent of those used in the First World War', which Hitler had requested – for there was not enough ammunition for this, but as heavy a barrage as the Allied troops had yet endured.

From beyond 'The Flyover' the artillery of VI Corps, numbering 432 guns, replied with equal force. For half an hour the air was rent with the deafening sound of exploding shells and filled with clouds of smoke. Then at half past six the infantry attacks began. Six separate diversionary attacks were made on the American 3rd Division; while the 4th Parachute Division assaulted the British with such force that it broke through the lines of the 56th Division and penetrated behind them for a distance of almost two miles.

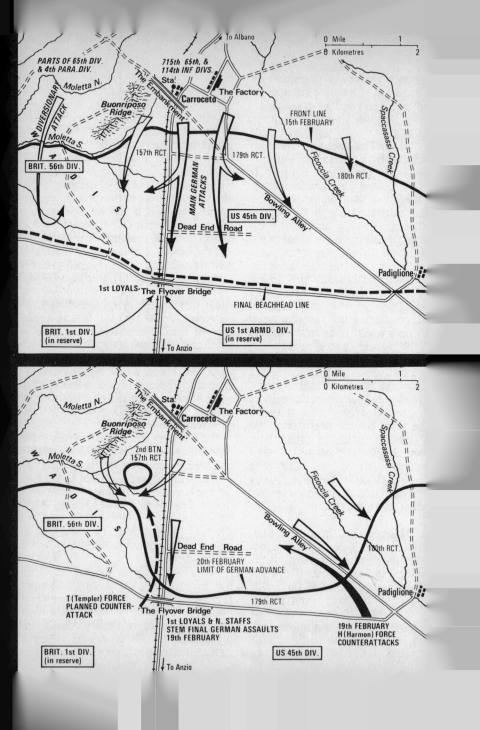

Map 1 (top):

To Albano

0 Mile 1
0 Kilometres 2

PARTS OF 65th DIV. & 4th PARA.DIV.

715th 65th, & 114th INF DIVS.

Moletta N.

The Embankment

Sta.

Carroceto

The Factory

Buonriposo Ridge

W

DIVERSIONARY ATTACK

157th RCT

179th RCT.

FRONT LINE 15th FEBRUARY

Spaccasassi Creek

Moletta S.

A

D

I

S

BRIT. 56th DIV.

MAIN GERMAN ATTACKS

US 45th DIV.

Dead End Road

Bowling Alley

Ficoccia Creek

180th RCT.

Padiglione

1st LOYALS The Flyover Bridge

FINAL BEACHHEAD LINE

BRIT. 1st DIV. (in reserve)

US 1st ARMD. DIV. (in reserve)

To Anzio

Map 2 (bottom):

0 Mile 1
0 Kilometres 2

Moletta N.

The Embankment

Sta.

Carroceto

The Factory

Buonriposo Ridge

2nd BTN. 157th RCT.

Spaccasassi Creek

Moletta S.

W

A

D

I

S

BRIT. 56th DIV.

Dead End Road

20th FEBRUARY LIMIT OF GERMAN ADVANCE

Bowling Alley

Ficoccia Creek

180th RCT.

179th RCT.

Padiglione

T (Templer) FORCE PLANNED COUNTER-ATTACK

The Flyover Bridge

1st LOYALS & N. STAFFS STEM FINAL GERMAN ASSAULTS 19th FEBRUARY

19th FEBRUARY H (Harmon) FORCE COUNTERATTACKS

BRIT. 1st DIV. (in reserve)

US 45th DIV.

To Anzio

But this, too, was a diversionary attack. The main assault fell with fearful force upon the American 179th and 157th Regimental Combat Teams in the centre of the Allied line. Both sides suffered crippling losses as the Germans forced their way between the American regiments and drove them both back for almost a mile. In particular the German troops who were given the task of advancing from 'The Factory' in the open were cut apart by the Americans' rifle and machine-gun fire and by the Allied artillery which poured a torrent of shells onto the open ground southeast of Carroceto.

The Americans, though they too were badly mauled, though several of their forward positions were overrun, though pushed back south of 'The Factory', held firm before the final beachhead line. But the much vaunted Lehr Regiment which Mackensen and Kesselring had unwillingly put in the vanguard of the attack eventually gave way. When most of its officers had been killed or wounded, the men faltered, refused to go on, then turned away from the fight. In Kesselring's dismissive words, they were 'thrown back disgracefully'. He blamed himself bitterly for having accepted them as a crack regiment and having entrusted to them so vital a task. 'Even though the Infantry Demonstration Regiment was put to me as a crack one,' he wrote in his memoirs, 'I should not have accepted this just on mere hearsay, but should have known a home defence unit with no fighting experience could not stand up to a major action. Another drawback was that the assault was fixed to begin at a very late hour, as the regiment, being unfamiliar with the terrain, could only properly attack in daylight.'

It was only the Lehr Regiment, however, that failed to fight well. Elsewhere along the front the Germans had gained ground. They had advanced across the forward positions of the 157th Regimental Combat Team and of the 167th Brigade of the 56th (London) Division and had driven both the Americans and the British back. Several companies of infantry had penetrated the front further west and pushed deep behind the lines. After dark a far stronger force of the 715th Division infiltrated between the 157th and 179th Regimental Combat Teams and blasted the American tanks and infantry off the Anzio-Albano road south of Carroceto, opening up a vital gap in the very centre of the Allied line.

At daylight the next morning, 17th February, another powerful attack, led by nearly forty dive bombers of the Luftwaffe, was launched into this gap in a determined attempt to split the Allied front wide open. Infantry and tanks of the 715th, 65th and 114th Divisions poured forward out of 'The Factory' and down the main road; while a simultaneous assault was made down the farm track that led from Carroceto to Padiglione.

Soon the two strong attacks appeared to be succeeding: the Allied front was indeed cracking open, the gap in the centre was being forced wide enough to admit the armour which Mackensen was holding in reserve until there was room enough for it to manoeuvre. Well inside the gap on the main road, three Grenadier Regiments and German infantry supported by tanks lashed out to their left against the 2nd Battalion of the 179th Regimental Combat Team and crushed it by weight of numbers. The survivors of this Battalion attempted to reform along a farm track about a mile in front of 'The Flyover'; but neither they nor the threatened 3rd Battalion seemed capable of holding out much longer and resisting the German onslaught which had already torn so gaping a hole in the middle of the Allies' front.

At this perilous moment – it was now about 09.00 hours on the 17th – the Allied air force came to VI Corps' rescue. As the full power of the artillery of VI Corps and of the 45th Division, supported by four batteries of 90mm anti-aircraft guns and the fire of two cruisers, opened up upon

Anti-aircraft watch in the hills

the Germans in the gap, every available aircraft of XII Air Support Command was sent flying to Anzio. 1,100 tons of bombs were dropped during 531 sorties. Never before in the war had such a weight of bombs been dropped in direct support of an army.

Yet, for all the density of the storm of high explosives on their positions, for all the temporary damage done to the men's nerves, the German attacks continued as relentlessly as before. Fourteen battalions supported by tanks pushed their way still further down the road to within a mile of 'The Flyover'; to the east of the road a counterattack by a Regiment of the 1st Amoured Division failed to retake any of the lost ground; to the west of it the Germans all but surrounded a battalion of the 157th Regiment. On the far right of the American 45th Division, the 180th Regimental Combat Team now also came under attack, while German tanks were threatening

'The Flyover' which two of them had almost reached before being stopped by anti-tank guns. In an effort to prevent a German breakthrough across 'The Flyover' and hence across the last defence line, part of the British 1st Division was called out of reserve to support the hard-pressed Americans. General Penney had not waited for this order, having already despatched the 1st Loyals to the area of 'The Flyover'.

At this critical moment, General Truscott, whose 3rd Division had been spared the main German attack, arrived at Corps Headquarters in response to a message from General Clark instructing him to assume the responsibility of deputy-commander. General Lucas, harassed and gloomy, had already ordered a counterattack when Truscott arrived. The American 1st Armoured Division had been told to drive straight up the Anzio-Albano road to do what it could to help the 157th Regimental Combat Team; and the 45th Infantry Division

112

was to make a night attack in support of the 179th. But there seemed to Truscott little faith at Corps Headquarters that either of these counterattacks would have the required results. The Headquarters, in fact, was overcast by a 'pall-like gloom'.

The pessimism was not unjustified. The 1st Armoured Division's tanks could not move off the main road because of the sogginess of the ground; they could not advance along it because of the heavy enemy gun fire. They failed to reach the 157th Regimental Combat Team, and were forced back behind 'The Flyover'.

Nor did the 45th Infantry Division's counterattack succeed any better. It was led by the 3rd Battalion of the 157th Regimental Combat Team, a battalion which had not suffered so many casualties as the other two in the Team. But it had been engaged most of the day nevertheless; and its men were tired and dispirited by their recent retreat. They managed to advance for about three-quarters of a

mile beyond 'The Flyover'; but having reached a track that extended eastwards from the main road here, a track which had become known as the 'Dead End Road', they came up against large, fresh forces of German troops lining up for a dawn attack. Against such troops the tired Americans were powerless. By dawn no news had reached Divisional headquarters from the 179th, and it was feared there that they would have to be 'written off'.

That day, 18th February, the Germans made what they expected would be a final effort to break the enemy front. There had been some discussion in the night as to whether the attack should be called off. Already fearfully heavy losses had been incurred; nearly every battalion had been reduced almost to the size of a company. Mackensen doubted that success was any longer within his grasp. But his Chief of Staff considered it 'would be folly to break off now', while Kesselring, well aware of what the Führer would demand, insisted that the fight should continue. They had already beaten an enormous dent in the Allied front two and a half miles wide and over a mile deep. They had lost great numbers of men and tanks in doing so, but they now had the necessary springboard for their last assault, and still considerable forces with which to make it.

Kesselring was anxious to make that assault as soon as possible, and with sufficient power to ensure an early success; for although the dent in the Allied line was, indeed, a big one, the thousands of German troops concentrated inside it, as well as hundreds of vehicles, made highly vulnerable targets for the enemy artillery. Fortunately it was another rainy morning, and there would be little danger from the air.

In the rain the exhausted British and American troops waited for the next attack. To the left, on the western shoulder of the dent in the Allied line, was the 2nd Battalion of the 157th Regimental Combat Team, less one company that had been driven back towards 'The Flyover'. The other companies, commanded by Lieutenant-Colonel Laurence C Brown, were established in a group of caves and gullies in the 'wadi' country south of Buonriposo Ridge cut off both from the British 45th Division on their left and from the troops around 'The Flyover' in their rear. The other shoulder of the dent, the right or eastern shoulder, was held by the 2nd Battalion of the 180th Regimental Combat Team. Along the bottom of the dent, eastwards from 'The Flyover', were the 1st Loyals and 179th Regimental Combat Teams. Behind them stood General Penney's 1st Division. But General Penney was no longer with it; he had been wounded, and Gerald Templer had had to take over.

Again on the 18th, as on the previous days, the German attacks hammered at the Allied centre, maintaining a savage artillery barrage on 'The Flyover' bridge and the road that ran over it. Tanks rumbled down the 'Bowling Alley' and along the main road, swarms of infantry rushed the posi-

The discomforts of battle. *Left:* A German soldier lives in a hole in the ground as protection against Allied bombers. *Above:* Synthetic fog created by American chemical engineers throughout daylight hours to conceal all military activities

tions of the 179th Regimental Combat Team and the isolated company of the 157th in front of 'The Flyover', pushing through to the Loyals. The American troops on both shoulders came under heavy attack. The 180th Regimental Combat Team on the eastern shoulder was forced to give ground, but held on north of Padiglione; the isolated 157th in its caves and gullies in the 'wadi' country held out grimly, too. All day the fighting raged while casualties on both sides mounted, the Germans suffering fearful losses as the Allied artillery sent wave after wave of shells over the lines.

At Corps Headquarters, Truscott urged Lucas to throw in his remaining reserves in a vigorous counter-attack before the beachhead was swamped. But Lucas still hesitated; and it was not until Mark Clark arrived and strongly advocated a 'counter-attack against the flanks of the salient' that the decision was taken.

While detailed plans for this counter-attack were being made, the Germans made yet another effort to break through the Allied lines to the sea.

As tanks and infantry battered at both the shoulders where the 157th and 180th Regimental Combat Teams were still bravely and stubbornly holding on, the main attack was launched down the main road once more against the 179th Regimental Combat Team and the Loyals. After ferocious fighting and the deaths of hundreds more soldiers, the battle was still undecided: the Allied line had been further dented but it had not yet finally broken.

In the early hours of the morning of 19th February, the Germans made their supreme effort to break it. Shortly before dawn they attacked again with a desperate courage, overrunning a company of the Loyals and seeming on the verge of storming past 'The Flyover' at last. Every available man, cooks and drivers, mechanics and storemen, clerks, even men from the Docks Operating Companies, were brought up from the rear to stem the tide.

Meanwhile the Allied counterattacks were going in. On the right a force known as Force H under General Harmon, comprising the 30th Infantry Regiment and the 6th Armoured Infantry Regiment with tanks from the 1st Armoured Division, had been given the task of attacking up the 'Bowling Alley' towards the eastern end of 'Dead End Road'. On the left, Force T under General Templer, consisting of the 169th Brigade of the 56th Division which had just landed at Anzio, was to move north from 'The Flyover' towards the isolated companies of Colonel Brown's Battalion of the 157th Regimental Combat Team, south of Buonriposo Ridge.

While the battle raged at 'The Flyover', the men of General Harmon's Force H prepared for their attack outside Padiglione. They were moving into position around the village when General Harmon was summoned to bring them back immediately to 'The Flyover' when a German breakthrough across the road now seemed imminent and inescapable. Harmon strongly objected. By the time he got back to 'The Flyover' all might be over there; his men had marched miles through the most difficult country in the darkness to reach Padiglione. Surely it would be better to use them as originally planned and hope that the Loyals and the 179th Combat Team would be able to hold out until his counterattack took effect. Corps Headquarters gave way; but then there was another complication. It was reported that an American battalion was stranded somewhere along the 'Bowling Alley', surrounded by Germans and still fighting hard to keep them at bay. This battalion was in the very centre of the area due shortly to be blasted by an artillery barrage as a prelude to the counterattack.

The decision was a fearful one for Harmon to have to make. If he stopped the barrage and delayed the counterattack, it might mean the collapse of the entire beachhead defences; if he allowed it to open he might be responsible for the slaughter of unknown numbers of his fellow-countrymen. But it seemed to him on reflection that really he had no choice. He gave the order for the guns to open fire.

To his relief he discovered when his infantry advanced that the American battalion had already retired before the barrage began. He also discovered that, although the enemy were still in considerable numbers between Padiglione and 'The Factory', they had been badly shaken by the barrage and had tired themselves out by their continuous exertions over the past twenty-four hours. They were far from being the strong, well organised force that had begun the attack in such confidence. Harmon's infantry moved in against them and forced them back to the 'Dead End Road', taking over two hundred prisoners.

The crisis of the battle had passed. At 'The Flyover' the German attack, at the very moment when it seemed on the verge of triumph, had collapsed. The troops who had fought so bravely for so long could do no more. They began to fall back towards Carroceto, across the country known with horrid appropriateness as the Campo di Carne, the field of flesh. The Loyals, helped by the 2nd North Staffordshires, came forward to drive the German rearguard out of the ruined houses which they had occupied to cover the retreat. They were as successful as the Americans on their right had been. In the last

A lull in the fighting

Above: A medic deals with dead German machine gunners. *Below:* Battalion waits for the order to move to the front

stronghold a white sheet was pushed out over the rubble. A few Germans came out to surrender followed by larger and larger groups until they were coming over the road in their hundreds.

But the battle was not quite over yet. Colonel Brown's men of the 157th Regimental Combat Team still fought on, surrounded by Germans in the 'wadi' country, preventing any serious infiltration through the western shoulder of the salient. They had been fighting there now for four days and nights and could not be expected to hold on unaided any longer. The plight of Lieutenant Ralph L Niffenegger's platoon, as recorded in Martin Blumenson's admirable account of the battle (see Bibliography), was typical of many. At the moment when the German attack had begun on the morning of the 16th, Niffenegger had thirty riflemen under his command and a light machine-gun section of eight men and two guns. After undergoing the heaviest concentration of shelling they had 'probably ever endured', the platoon came under strong infantry attack. Their machine-gunners managed to kill about twenty of the advancing Germans, but when the attack was over four of Niffenegger's men were dead and six were wounded. Soon afterwards the depleted platoon was attacked again, and, although this attack too was beaten off, Niffenegger thought that 'a few more men and a few more minutes' would have led to his men being 'completely overrun'. By now one of his machine-guns was out of action through an overheated barrel; half his ammunition was exhausted; he had only twenty men left; his wounded could not be evacuated because the route to the battalion aid station was under fire; and he was surrounded. Another German attack resulted in the loss of a further eight men taken as prisoners. By the time he received orders to withdraw into the caves of the 'wadi' country where the rest of his battalion were holding out, Niffenegger had only six men left.

General Templer's T Force had been unable to start its counterattack as planned the night before, but one of its component parts, the 2/7th Battalion of the Queen's Royal Regiment of the 169th Brigade was now sent to Colonel Brown's relief.

The Queen's were soon in difficulties. They came up against overwhelmingly stronger forces of enemy troops, and used so much ammunition in fighting their way through them, that when they did eventually reach the Americans, they had little left, and no supporting weapons. Unless help came to them there was little hope of holding out after the Americans had gone.

The Americans left the next night, creeping out into the darkness in small groups in an attempt to slip through the net of troops that the Germans had built around them. Colonel Brown had had eight hundred men under his command when the battle had begun. Only two hundred of these managed to escape from the caves and reach the Allied lines, and of these half were wounded.

Soon it was the turn of the Queen's to fight their way out as best they could. Already the positions of their forward platoons had been overrun and neither supplies nor reinforcements could be got to the survivors. The weather was so bad that supplies could not be dropped to them from the air, and an attempt to relieve them by the other battalion of the Queen's in the Brigade, the 2/6th, had failed. Yet the Queen's held out for several days, uneasily watching the Germans closing in, harbouring what remained of their dwindling ammunition, firing only when not to fire meant death or capture. On 23rd February two entire companies were lost in an attack; but it was not until four days later that the last platoon was able to get away.

By then the Allies had gained a new confidence. In the five days of fighting between 16th and 20th February, they had lost another five thousand men to add to the fourteen thousand casualties already suffered before the German attack began. But the German casualties were known to be heavy too – they were, in fact, about the same: five thousand men, most of them the result of the artillery concentrations. Also, VI Corps had gained a new commander in whom everyone had more confidence than General Lucas was capable of inspiring.

On 22nd February, General Clark had told Lucas that he was to be replaced by his deputy, General Truscott. Lucas, naturally, had taken the news badly. As the recent battle had died away, he had sent a message to the troops: 'Swell work today – keep after them.' He felt that this decision to consolidate his forces on the beaches and to harbour his resources had all along been justified, and now he was to be dismissed after the great German counterattack, which he had so long expected, had been broken. He condemned Clark for giving way to the British from whom, he suspected, most of the criticism of him came.

His suspicions, in fact, were well founded. On 15th February, Alexander had complained to General Brooke in London about Lucas's lack of initiative and drive and had asked him to consult Eisenhower. Already Churchill, 'in the depths of gloom over Italy', had expressed his grave doubts to Brooke 'as to whether Lucas was handling this landing efficiently'. Brooke had 'some job quietening him down again. Unfortunately this time [there were] reasons for uneasiness'.

On 16th February, Alexander repeated his complaints about Lucas to General Clark. 'You know the position is serious,' Alexander said to him. 'We may be pushed back into the sea. That would be very bad for both of us, and you would certainly be relieved of your command.'

Clark asked Alexander where exactly he had got all his information about Lucas's alleged incapacity. And after detailing what he considered to be the Corps commander's failings, Alexander admitted that his criticisms rested mainly on the evidence of General Penney, commander of the British Division. Clark riposted by claiming that not only Lucas, but all three American divisional commanders had as little confidence in Penney himself. However, Clark agreed that Lucas's conduct was not above criticism; it might be best to replace him; but it must be done in as kindly a way as possible.

Clark broke the news gently. Personally, he assured Lucas, he had not lost confidence in him; he believed that he had acted correctly in not dashing off for the Alban Hills and leaving the Corps so extended that it was liable to be destroyed; he thought that he had done everything that could have been expected of him. But he 'could no longer resist the pressure' from higher up, and Lucas would have to leave Anzio. There was no question of disgrace. In fact, he was to be promoted. On his return to the United States he was to assume command of the Fourth Army.

Lucas was not much comforted by Clark's kindness. He felt strongly that he had directed the operation in the only way that it could have been directed; and now that his methods were beginning to pay off, now that he was 'winning something of a victory', he was being fired. He never recovered from the blow to his pride and self-respect. He was already unwell, tired out by the responsibilities of command. He died a few years later.

General Truscott had not wanted to succeed him. He was quite content to be his adviser; but Clark impressed upon him that the move was essential to the restoration of Anglo-American accord, and Truscott accepted the verdict and entered upon his duties with refreshing energy. The British liked and respected Truscott as much as they had distrusted Lucas; and when an English deputy commander was appointed, Major-General Evelegh, whom the Americans in their turn liked, the growing discord between the Allies was dispelled.

Truscott knew that the relative quiet of the few days that followed his appointment was but the prelude to a new attack. The expected assault came on 29th February.

Kesselring and Mackensen had been unwilling to make it. Both of them believed that if their original plan had not been countermanded by Hitler, the battle for Anzio would by now have been won. Had the troops been sent forward on a wide front employing the infiltration tactics which had been so successful in the earlier engagements, they must certainly have reached the sea. As it was, the narrow thrust had been broken by the stubbornness of the enemy's resistance, above all by the remorseless weight of their accurate artillery fire. The troops – with the exception of the Lehr Regiment – could not have done more to make the Führer's plan succeed; but now that it had failed, they had not enough strength left to strike the final crushing blow which Hitler was demanding. Kesselring himself, far less optimistic now than he had been the week before, had little confidence in the success of this final blow; yet, since Hitler demanded it, it must be made; and even if it did not succeed in its immediate objective it might well make another deep dent in the beachhead, a dent which so constricted it that artillery fire would make it impossible for the Allies to retain it.

So on the last day of February, another day of such bad weather that they could bring their tanks forward without interference from Allied aircraft, the Germans attacked once more. For a time it appeared that yet again the assault would fall in the centre; but the main attack was made not on the Albano-Anzio road and 'The Flyover', but on the Cisterna front against the American 3rd Division, now commanded by the aggressive Brigadier-General John WO'Daniel, known to his men as 'Iron Mike'.

Truscott was relieved that the attack fell here, for the 3rd Division was now the least tired in the Corps and had been reinforced to make up for the casualties that had been suffered in the early days of the fighting. It had also been given additional anti-tank guns, and a battalion from the 1st American Armoured Regiment had been placed under its command.

Before dawn the 3rd Division called for an intensive barrage on the Germans obviously forming up for an attack in their sector. The call was immediately answered by a fierce concentration of fire; but despite this discouragement, three German divisions moved forcefully into the attack at daylight.

Immediately a company of the 509th Parachute Battalion was overrun and all its officers but one and all its men but twenty-two became casualties or prisoners of war. To the right of the 509th, the German 362nd Division, supported by tanks of the 26th Panzer Grenadier and Hermann Göring Divisions, drove in the centre of the 3rd Division's front. And further still to the east, the 715th Division and the 16th SS Panzer Grenadier Division pushed past the forward positions of the 504th Parachute Infantry Regiment. But none of these penetrations went deep.

Checked by minefields, by accurate American small-arms fire and artillery, and by the brave resistance of American troops, the Germans faltered after gaining little ground. The attacks were renewed the next day, but they were marked by none of the spirit and determination that had characterised the earlier fighting.

On 2nd March the weather cleared and Allied medium and fighter-bombers were able to take off again. Escorted by 176 P-38 Lightnings and P-47 Thunderbolts, nearly 350 B24 Liberators and B17 Flying Fortresses dropped over six hundred tons of bombs along the front and on German concentrations around Cisterna, Campoleone, Carroceto and Velletri. This ferocious bombardment marked the end of the first stage of the Anzio battle. In fact, Kesselring had already decided before it began to call off his final attack which had cost him more than three thousand casualties and thirty tanks. By 4th March his troops were digging in, and a new phase of the battle began.

Night artillery barrage

Lull

'The Beachhead has become a Death's Head.' German propaganda leaflet dropped on the Allied troops at Anzio, March 1944.

After more than a month of bombardment both from the sea and the air, there were few buildings anywhere on the beachhead that were not at least partially in ruins. Almost every night the port and anchorage had been attacked; and for all the efforts of the naval gunners and the men in the anti-aircraft batteries, aircraft frequently succeeded in getting through the defences to drop their loads of high explosives and radio-controlled bombs.

In all during the Anzio operation the

Royal Navy lost two light cruisers, three destroyers, the hospital ship *St David*, three LSTs and one LCI. 429 sailors were killed or wounded. The United States Navy lost 326 men killed and wounded, two minesweepers, two Liberty ships, five landing craft and one LST. Nearly all these losses were suffered during air raids. Attacks by German and Italian E Boats accounted for the loss of but one LST; and a raid by twenty-three Marder 'human torpedoes' was entirely unsuccessful, no Allied craft at all being sunk and ten of the Marders being destroyed or captured.

The Luftwaffe did not limit its attention to the port. Nowhere on the entire

beachhead was safe from attack, although the whole area was concealed from view for most of the town by clouds of artificial fog that hung heavily in the air, greasy and evil-smelling. Ammunition depots, petrol dumps, equipment stores, road junctions were all attacked; and the nearby casualty clearing stations and hospitals all necessarily suffered. 'The wounded lay ... in their sodden, filthy clothes,' wrote a British medical officer: 'greatcoats, pullovers, battle-dresses, all of the thickest, soaked, caked, buried in mud and blood; with the ghastly pale faces, shuddering, shivering with the cold of the February nights and their great wounds... I grew to hate that combination of yellow pad, bloody, dirty brown bandage, and mud-darkened skin... Some were unconscious, these chiefly head wounds, whose loud snoring breathing distinguished them; some (too many; far too many) were carried in dying, with gross combinations of shattered limbs, protrusions of intestines and brains... Some lay quiet and still, with legs drawn up – the penetrating wounds of the abdomen. Some were carried in sitting up on the stretchers, gasping and coughing, shot through the lungs.' Many of them had survived only to be killed by a bomb as they lay waiting for treatment or recovering from an operation. In the same week the American 33rd Field Hospital, the 56th Evacuation Hospital, the 3rd Division Clearing Station and the 62nd Medical Battalion were all attacked, and the casualties included two nurses killed.

Grimly aware that a not too painful wound – so urgently hoped for on other fronts – might not bring release from the danger, fear and discomfort of Anzio, the British and American soldiers were further disheartened by the demoralizing propaganda that came over so persistently from behind the German lines. To many soldiers, of course, this propaganda meant nothing, to some it was a source of amusement, even pleasure, but to others it was as

Supplies are unloaded

dispiriting and provocative as the Germans intended it to be.

Two voices, broadcasting from Rome, were relayed to the Allies every night. One of them, the voice of a man, warned of the futility of further resistance, of the dangers and horrors to come: 'Have you heard about Private Fox? He went on patrol and stepped on a *Schuh* mine. Nasty things, *Schuh* mines. All his guts were blown away. But he went on living another twelve hours. You should have heard him yelling... so easy, boys. There's danger ahead!'

The other voice, coaxing and sensuous, was that of an apparently young and, one presumed, pretty girl. She told her listeners, between gramophone records of dance music and jazz, all about the way their wives and girlfriends were behaving with men who had had more sense than to join the army, who were 'getting it in all over the place', just as the soldiers would live to do again, if only they saw sense and gave themselves up. Two men of the 179th had seen the light, she said, and were now out of the firing line, finished with fighting, looking forward to the happy days ahead when the war would be over, won by Germany. They weren't badly treated now, either. 'Think it over,' she suggested. 'Think it over.'

As well as the broadcasts, there were the propaganda leaflets. These were fired over in shells that scattered them all over the forward areas. Some gave tips on how to make yourself ill enough to fool the doctor, to poison your blood so that you would be sent back to a base hospital, to feign shell shock. Others, directed against the British, sought to undermine their confidence in the Americans, to sow distrust of their commanders: 'WHAT IT MEANS TO BE PUT UNDER AMERICAN COMMAND YOUR FORCES ARE FINDING OUT' was the heading of one such pamphlet. It went on: 'The "accomplishments" of this American leadership are indeed typically American: operations were insufficiently prepared and led to the most

dreadful reverses for your troops. Your picked units were carelessly thrown into the battle. CERTAINLY THE YANKS PLAYED YOU A NASTY TURN.'

The other side of this pamphlet reminded the British that they were up against determined German troops, not Italians now: 'As gallant soldiers you have had the occasion to become acquainted with courage and the grit of your German opponent.

'You know how well the Germans stood up in battle, although they were always inferior to you in numbers. But you know well enough what it means when the Germans are numerically equal to your own forces or even superior.

'In the face of insurmountable odds a thousand men of crack British Guards surrendered.

'If they were forced to do so, then it is not dishonourable for you to lay down arms in case you are facing nothing but certain death.

'General Clark certainly played you a dirty Yankee trick! And who has got to bear the consequences?'

The theme of many of these pamphlets designed to undermine Anglo-American relations was the sexual behaviour of the doughboy in England where, paid so much better than the British soldier, he was seducing every woman he could lay his hands on. 'You are so different' was the caption to one leaflet depicting a girl lying on her bed, gazing excitedly at a predatory American sergeant. Another showed an American private knotting his tie while a naked girl, smiling contentedly as she sits on a rumpled bed, rolls on a silk stocking. A third, with the question 'And what about you?' above a solitary grave, was captioned: 'British soldiers! You are fighting and dying far away from your country while the Yanks are putting up their tents in Merry Old England. They've got lots of money, and loads of time to chase after your women.'

In the pamphlets directed at the American troops the villain, who enjoyed American women and American

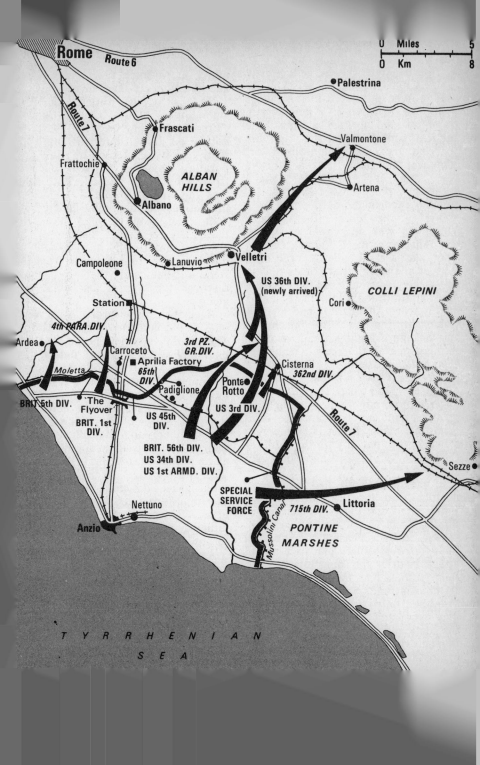

life while the doughboy was away, was the archetypal character in German propaganda, the fat, rich, greedy Jew: 'It must be nice to carry on the kind or war portrayed in the revues on Upper Broadway; a long-legged, grape-breasted girl in a cute little uniform squeals "Bum!" – and the poor, hungry, lousy, demoralized Germans wet their pants and reach for the sky... Why it's enough to make a decent guy puke himself sick, all this mucking revue and newspaper crap.'

One of the more effective later pamphlets was addressed to British and American troops alike. On the front was a skull superimposed on a map of the beachhead. In its hollow eye-sockets were marked the towns of Anzio and Nettuno; around its grinning mouth were Allied ships and aircraft sinking in the sea. 'The Beachhead has become a Death's Head', warned the message on the back. 'The beachhead is going to be the big blow against the Germans. Wasn't that the slogan when the Allied troops landed? Today, exactly three months of hard fighting have passed and you can now celebrate this event. But it is still merely a beachhead, paved with the skulls of thousands of British and American soldiers!'

If the beachhead had become a death's head for the Allies, it also represented for the Germans a continuing drain on their resources. Kesselring and Mackensen had flung all their reserves into their determined attack to drive the Allies into the sea; their troops had fought with initial confidence and continuing bravery. They had failed and their energy was now exhausted. There was nothing for the commanders to do now but to wait, to conserve their forces for defence against the Allied offensive which was bound to come in the spring.

General Siegfried Westphal left for Germany to bear this unpalatable news to the Führer who would not accept reality if faced with nothing more than a written report, who might not accept it even when told by one of his most expert generals that there was now no possibility of a continued counterattack at Anzio in the face of Allied superiority in artillery and aircraft.

On his arrival, Hitler's Chief of Operations Staff, Colonel-General Alfred Jodl, strongly advised Westphal not to ask for an interview until the blow had been softened by some preparatory remarks by the Chief of Operations Staff himself. But Hitler was no more prepared to accept intimations of impending defeat from Jodl than from anyone else. His troops were being slandered; he ordered that twenty men should be flown to him for interview from the Italian front and then he would discover for himself just what was going on.

Nevertheless, he agreed to see Westphal at Berchtesgaden on 6th March. The painful interview lasted for three hours. Westphal's patient, determined arguments were frequently interrupted by Hitler who was roused to fury at every suggestion that his army at Anzio would have to go onto the defensive, that his hopes of an overwhelming victory were now but illusions. Although he persisted in his belief that all he needed to solve his present problems was a victory, he came at the end with great emotion to admit, so Westphal reported, 'that he knew how great was the war weariness which afflicted the people and the Wehrmacht'.

As month followed month at Anzio, war weariness became more and more noticeable, too, amongst the Allied troops. Forced to settle down to a form of static trench warfare characteristic of the First World War, they grumbled miserably as they dug themselves down deep into the mud.

The defence line remained virtually the same as it had been at the end of the great German counterattack on 20th February. There were some alterations in the line, but they were minor ones. On 3rd March for instance, the Americans regained Ponte Rotto on the Cisterna-Nettuno road, after a

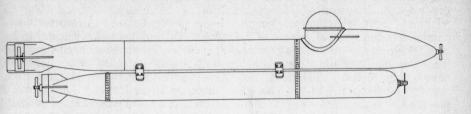

The Germans built several classes of midget submarines, mainly for use against invasion fleets. They were not very successful, however. The Marder type illustrated was similar to the Neger type, but could run submerged. *Displacement:* 5 tons. *Dimensions:* 26 by 1¾ by 3½ feet. *Power/speed:* 12 hp/20 knots. *Radius of action:* 30 miles at 3 knots. *Crew:* 1. The craft itself was a torpedo from which the warhead had been removed and replaced by a new section carrying a cockpit and controls. A conventional torpedo was slung beneath this

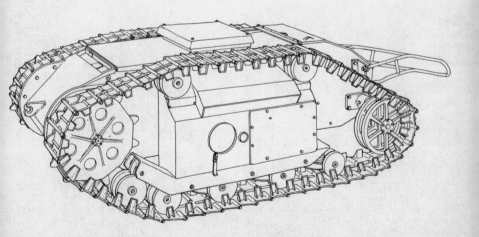

One of the 'wonder' weapons produced by the Wehrmacht, the 'Goliath' miniature tank was an abject failure. Designed to advance inconspicuously against Allied troops and then be detonated, the vehicle was too easily spotted and halted by Allied small arms' fire. Powered by either a small petrol or electric engine, the speed of the Goliath was between five and twelve miles per hour, carrying a 200-pound explosive charge. It was steered through trailing wires, and had a range of 2,000 feet. One of the reasons for its failure was its height, which was about two feet

strong and well conducted counter-attack; and there were frequent small changes to the line where it ran through the 'wadi' country and where forward positions were constantly changing hands. But the general outline of the beachhead stayed the same, stretching from the mouth of the Moletta – held now by the British 5th Division commanded by General Gregson-Ellis (replacing the 56th which had gone back into reserve on the southern front) – dipping into the line of the dent by 'The Flyover', held by the 1st and 45th Divisions, passing in front of Cisterna, where the American 3rd Division under General O'Daniel was still in control, and down to the Mussolini Canal, held by the Special Service Force, a force of Americans and Canadians commanded by General R T Frederick.

The American Rangers and the para-troops had been withdrawn from the beachhead and had been replaced by the 34th Infantry Division which, with the 1st Armoured Division, was in reserve. To be held in reserve, however, did not necessarily mean to be out of fire, for the beachhead stretched only seventeen miles or so along the coast and it was but seven miles from Anzio up to the front by 'The Flyover'. Nowhere could be considered entirely safe, other than places such as the network of catacombs and cellars which had been constructed over the centuries in the volcanic soil beneath the now ruined streets of Nettuno.

In this constricted area, any part of which might suddenly come under attack, the organisation and supply of the Allied army had to be maintained, communications had to be kept open, all the needs of the fighting soldiers to be met. 'This army is like a peacock,' Churchill once said to General Brooke when complaining about the number of vehicles needed to maintain it, 'it

A Goliath that was disabled before reaching its target

is all tail.' 'The peacock,' Brooke had replied, 'would be a very ill-balanced bird without its tail.'

The tail at Anzio appeared to be in constant motion as DUKWs moved backwards and forwards across the harbour between the Liberty ships and the shore, as trucks rattled through the streets to the petrol and ammunition dumps, as convoys moved up the roads towards the forward areas past red-painted notices reading 'DANGER SHELLING. MAKE NO DUST.'

Already by the beginning of February the port was handling eight LSTs, eight LCTs and fifteen LCIs at the same time, while every day six LSTs, each carrying fifty loaded trucks, discharged 1,500 tons of cargo onto the beaches and took aboard fifty empty trucks for the return journey to Naples. As darkness fell, the tail became still and quiet; and then the front, which throughout the day had been quiet in its turn, came to life again, and the silence would be shattered by the intermittent rattle of Spandau and Bren-gun fire or the crash of mortar bombs, and the darkness would be broken by the glare of Verey lights.

Some parts of the front were very much more active and dangerous than others. The most westerly sector north of Anzio where the British 5th Division held the mouth of the Moletta was, for instance, relatively calm. Although the forward platoons here were less than fifty yards from the German lines, there was rarely any firing.

Further to the east, in the 'wadi' country, however, where the Germans held the higher ground overlooking the Allied positions, where the men had to crawl about in the holes and gullies keeping out of sight, there was activity almost every night. Indeed, the Allies were obliged to send out frequent patrols, for the Germans, commanding all the vantage points on the higher ground, would otherwise have slowly eroded the line by night infiltration and limited probing attacks.

Every 'wadi' had its own name. There were 'The North Lobster Claw' and 'The South Lobster Claw', 'The Culvert', 'The Starfish', 'The Boot' and 'The Fortress'. And it was to 'The Fortress' that a twenty-year-old officer in the Rifle Brigade, Raleigh Trevelyan, then serving with a battalion in the 5th Division, was sent in the first week of March. He found the position of the platoon he was sent to on the edge of a small, deep valley tangled with undergrowth, which ran, like a fissure caused by some primeval earthquake, through the flat grassland – one of the formidable 'wadis'.

The enemy was about seventy yards away, but bushes seemed to block the view everywhere. 'One advantage of being so close to the Germans,' he related in an account that vividly evokes the character of the fighting at Anzio, 'was that we were within the minimum range of their mortars. Snipers and hand grenades were the main worry, not counting shells falling short and air-bursts. All night long the artillery and mortars of both sides kept up a non-stop barrage... Sometimes the explosions were close enough for us to see shreds of flame spreading upwards in the dark, and the shrapnel would come hissing at us from all sides.'

There was a heavy cloying smell everywhere, Trevelyan immediately noticed; but it was not until daylight that he discovered its causes: the empty tins of bully beef and stew that had been thrown into the bushes. In addition, the previous platoon had been none too particular about the disposal of human excreta... Nor had they bothered to bury the German corpses that lay strewn about the undergrowth in the platoon area and had been lying there for a fortnight. There were about two inches of brown water at the bottom of the trench that Trevelyan shared with his batman.

Week in and week out, with occasional rests out of the line, Trevelyan and his platoon defended this part of the front, often cold and more than occasionally wet, sometimes exchang-

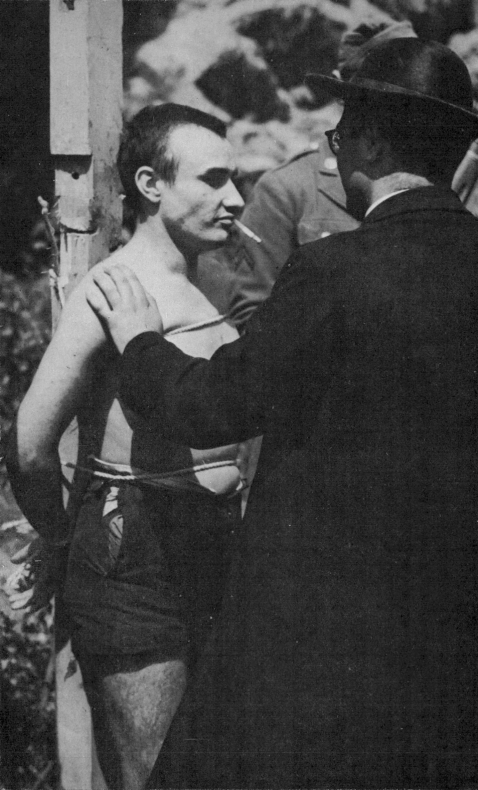

ing positions with other platoons, sometimes going out on patrol, putting wire across open gaps, digging new trenches, erecting booby traps, fighting off enemy patrols, shooting at Germans who unwarily came out of cover, enduring mortar and rifle grenade attacks, repaying the enemy in kind. For just over a fortnight at the end of March and the beginning of April, they moved further west to a different part of the front where there were no 'wadis', where the enemy were six or seven hundred yards away, and where platoon headquarters were sited beneath a cowshed which American Engineers had made into 'a real masterpiece' of a fortress, reinforced with sandbags. The cowshed was full of American supplies, infinitely superior to the supplies to which the British soldier was accustomed – pineapple juice, sweet corn, tinned butter, tins of sliced turkey Swiss Gruyere, California peaches, sweets and chewing-gum, coffee powder, cigarettes 'and what would be at least a year's ration of sugar for one person at home'. The British soldiers, used to an unvarying diet of tinned meat, tinned fruit, biscuits, tea and sometimes rice pudding, were as gratified as they were envious.

Then they returned to 'The Fortress' where it was still 'so bewildering the way our own and the Jerries' positions are so interwoven. There is no hard and fast straight line as the front between us. Moreover the Jerries still seem to control the main vantage points, and roughly speaking they are dug in round three of the four sides of the batallion area. The men keep on asking why we don't press forward and drive the enemy back – any risk is better than our present conditions. The answer is that there are more 'wadis' beyond and at the expense of much blood we would only be in exactly the same predicament, but with lengthier lines of communication.'

Yet there were constant rumours of

Execution for a condemned Italian spy

an imminent march on Rome; and an air of uneasiness hung in the air. 'It's not unlikely,' Trevelyan thought, 'that the Germans may get windy and decide to mop up some of our outlying posts, of which mine is a perfect victim... It's a regular feature of one's existence at the front that the high-ups should keep us entirely in the dark about what's going on, particularly as regards the disposition of our own troops. A fine example of the shambles that this can cause was the other night when we arrived at Michele, a place near the Elbow.'

The Germans had got wind of the changeover and as the platoon came up onto an exposed ridge they were pinned down by heavy Spandau fire. It was a very dark night, so none of them could be picked out individually; but the men were frightened that they would be caught out there in a mortar bombardment. The only cover on the ridge was a shallow and narrow crawl trench, and down this men from the unit being relieved were crawling as fast as they could, making no secret of their desperate anxiety to get away as quickly as possible. 'At one moment we were jammed head to toe, completely immobile, with volleys of tracer like whip lashes a matter of inches overhead ... Six of my men were wounded. Someone had a bullet through his head and was screaming loudly. No one attempted to help as they passed him. I eased myself up, wondering what on earth to do, when stretcher bearers arrived. They stumbled over the hillside, waving their flag, but the fools didn't seem to realize that the Germans couldn't see a red cross in the dark – they were only attracting attention by wagging this large shape on the skyline. They were quickly mown down. Then more stretcher-bearers came, and the same thing happened.

'Porter was one of my wounded. I don't think he was badly hurt, but he cried out a great deal. When I tried to soothe him, he struck at me wildly, spitting like a jaguar. "Let me go, you – fool." He suddenly sprang up and bolted away into the night. I haven't heard if he survived.

'Porter's behaviour quite petrified the other members of his section. Although we had reached the end and were but a few yards from the Michele wadi, they refused to budge. So I had to go back and fetch each one singly. That meant five separate trips.

'When light came, I found my hands covered with blood – whether Porter's or from that other fellow who screamed so, I don't know.'

Quite a different kind of war was fought further west where the British 1st and American 45th Divisions defended the dented line by 'The Flyover'. The British positions on the embankment of 'The Flyover' dominated the German positions beyond, and there was consequently no need for patrols in the scarred and broken country, littered with the ruins and debris of war, where the savage battle of February had been fought. Instead, both sides of 'The Flyover' and the embankment itself were constantly bombarded by artillery fire, churning up still further the already tortured earth.

Away to the southeast, along the Mussolini Canal, yet another sort of warfare was being fought. Here the Americans and Canadians of the 1st Special Service Force fought on a long front, defending the high banks of the Canal that cut its way through the Pontine Marshes to the sea south of Borgo Piave. It was more easily defensible ground than the 'wadi' country; but the Force numbered scarcely more than a thousand men and they were stretched out thinly over ten miles of winding canal. A concentrated German attack was never expected in that sector, but to make it all the more unlikely, the men of the Special Service Force were required to fight a tirelessly aggressive campaign in the low, flat lands, beyond the banks of the Canal, to persuade the Germans, by repeated and powerful night attacks, that they held the line in far greater strength than they did.

They performed this task with spirit and accomplishment under the command of their General, RT Frederick, 'a slight, pale-faced man with a dapper black moustache', in the words of the war correspondent Wynford Vaughan-Thomas, 'which gave him the air of a bank clerk in a small branch office in the country, and the visitor to his dug-out headquarters near the Mussolini Canal would wonder if this was, indeed, the legendary Frederick, the outstanding battle leader of popular repute – until he began to talk.'

His men went out almost every night to raid the German outposts beyond the Canal, blowing up forward positions and headquarters far behind the front, sticking labels bearing a red arrow, which was their regimental emblem, on the walls of farmhouses or scrawling threats and warnings. When armoured support was made available to them they made their attacks by day; and before April was over they had driven several deep dents in the German line which remained permanently bent throughout the remainder of the time that the beachhead existed.

General Harmon was only too pleased to allow his tanks to be used in support of the Special Service Force. They were held in reserve in the Padiglione woods, and his men needed as much occupation as they could get, for the area came under regular artillery attack, and the men had begun to grumble that this was all they were there for – to draw the enemy's fire.

To keep them more fully occupied, the men were asked to invent devices that would help the troops get over the enemy's obstacles when the time came to break out of the beachhead. They produced various ideas which were developed and found workable. Most of them were designed to solve the problems of quickly overcoming the obstacles that the Germans had built in front of their positions and three of these seemed particularly promising. One was a kind of grap-

A patrol of the 1st Special Service Force in action

pling iron which could be fired from a tank across a barbed-wire fence and could then be winched back to clear a way through for the infantry. Another was a bridge which could be pushed forward by a tank across a ditch. The third was an adaptation of 'the snake', a long metal tube filled with explosives to within about fifty feet of the tank that towed it towards a minefield. At the edge of the mine-field, the tank wheeled round swinging 'the snake' across; the crew then detonated it by firing their machine-guns at it, thus blasting a clear path for the infantry.

Occupying their time by perfecting such devices, the men of the Armoured Division waited for the winter to pass and for the great breakout from the beachhead to begin. But April came, and the front remained as static as ever. Indeed, many of the troops felt that warfare at Anzio was taking on the character of a kind of set ritual. The harbour was bombed with mono- tonous regularity; 'Anzio Annie' con- tinued to rattle at intervals out of her railway tunnel and deliver her salvo of shells across the Allied front; infantry units came out of the line for a few days' rest and then went back into it again to occupy the positions with which they were becoming so sadly familiar.

The Germans, for their part, were quite as frustrated with the long stale- mate as the Allies were; and, as though in recognition of a common plight and shared predicament, a kind of sympathy had developed between the front-line troops of the opposing armies. Soldiers on both sides would often refrain from firing at each other when one of their number incautiously came out of his hole in the ground to stretch his cramped legs or to enjoy the sunshine in what he took to be a screened position. Once, when a British

ANZIO. By vocket?

While you are away,

soldier out on patrol trod on a *Schus-mine* and lost a foot and had to be abandoned in No-Man's land, German and British stretcher bearers under protection of their Red Cross flags went to collect him at the same time. They met beside the body of the wounded man where, after offering each other cigarettes, they tossed up to decide which of the two parties should carry him away. On another occasion a drunken American soldier stumbled through a minefield and into the German lines wearing a black top-hat which he had found in a ruined villa. The Germans treated him indulgently and, having secured the top-hat more securely on his head, turned him round and wished him luck on his homeward journey which he completed safely to the evident satisfaction of all concerned.

Yet, for all this intermittent *camaraderie*, for all the half-formed though widespread fear that Anzio was a forgotten theatre of war and that the stalemate would continue for as long as the war itself, no one who saw the docks at Anzio in May 1944 could seriously doubt that the breakout would come soon. Attacks by sea and from the air, and artillery bombardments from land had all alike failed to prevent vast stores of material, ammunition and supplies building up in the beachhead. Over half a million tons of supplies were landed at Anzio during the course of the operation, nearly eight thousand tons on one single day alone. At the height of its activity, the port was taking in a greater tonnage than all but six other ports in the world. Soon, surely, the wildcat which Churchill had hoped to throw ashore at Anzio would at last strike out, claw its way north, and play its expected part in the plans of the Allied High Command.

German propaganda leaflets were dropped to demoralise the soldiers. This one taunted the British with visions of life at home

These plans, if properly executed, might even bring the war to an end before the summer was over. For the Germans were to be assaulted from three directions at once. The Russians were to advance in the east; a new front was to be opened up in the west by a landing in Normandy; while the enemy was to be threatened also in the south by the British and American armies and their numerous Allies in Italy.

These armies, comprising Indian, Polish, French and African units, as well as British and American, were to begin the attack. And they were to begin it with such determination and force that the Germans would not merely be prevented from withdrawing their divisions from Italy to help stop the advance through France but would be thrown back across the Gustav Line, driven out of Rome, and overwhelmed on the plains to the north.

Alexander's offensive in Italy was to be timed so that Rome would be captured just before Operation Overlord began. The intention was to break through the right wing of the German Tenth Army, to drive both this army and the German Fourteenth Army north of Rome and to pursue them both vigorously. The British Eighth Army was to attack through the Liri Valley and advance to the east of Rome along the axis of Route 6, while, at the same time, the American Fifth Army was to make a parallel attack by way of the Ansonia defile, south of the Liri and Sacco Rivers. Then General Truscott's Corps in the Anzio beachhead would break out north towards Valmontone and throw itself across Route 6, thus closing the German Tenth Army's withdrawal route and simultaneously cutting off its supplies.

To ensure the success of the offensive on his western front, Alexander transferred as many units as could be spared from the Adriatic front to reinforce his divisions in the Garigliano, Liri Valley and Cassino sectors. In order to deceive the Germans as to

BRITISH SOLDIERS!

You are fighting against an opponent whom you know very well.

You are not facing Italians but Germans.

As gallant soldiers you have had occasion to become acquainted with the courage and the grit of your German opponent.

You know how well the Germans stood up in battle, although they were always inferior to you in number. But you know well enough what it means when the Germans are numerically equal to your own forces or even superior.

In the face of insurmountable odds a thousand men of crack British Guards surrendered.

If t h e y were forced to do so, then it is not dishonourable for you to lay down arms in case you are facing nothing but certain death.

General Clark certainly played you a dirty Yankee trick !
And who has got to bear the consequences?

where the attack was to fall, a cover plan was devised to persuade them that a second amphibious operation was being prepared, that the Allies would make a landing north of Rome at Civitavecchia. This cover plan entailed the simulation of intense activity at Salerno where Canadian wireless detachments transmitted messages which indicated that at least two divisions were training there. The area was marked with numerous Canadian corps signs, while in the Bay ships of the Royal Navy undertook what appeared to be practice landings. Simultaneously, reconnaissance aircraft flew up and down the coastline north of Rome, concentrating on Civitavecchia which was also the subject of intensive aerial photography.

Elaborate as were the measures taken to persuade the Germans that a landing north of Rome rather than an attack from the south was being prepared, no less thorough were the steps taken to ensure that the mass movement of troops and materials from the Adriatic to the western front, and the re-grouping of forces for an attack in the west, should pass unobserved. Troops were usually moved by night, and were brought into forward areas at the last possible moment, while vehicles continued to mill about the camps they had left as though they had not been moved at all. Dummy tanks made of wood and canvas were left behind in areas evacuated by armoured units. Screens were erected to conceal from the view of observers on Monte Cassino the lines of vehicles that wound their way along the road at its base. The jeep and mule tracks which were constructed in the mountains for the supply of II Polish Corps on either side of the Appenines were hidden from the enemy by camouflage nets stretched above them in the trees. New gun emplacements, ammunition and supply dumps, concentrations of tanks and guns were all

as carefully camouflaged.

The Allies' meticulous care in keeping the Germans unaware of their attentions was not taken in vain. By the beginning of May, the Eighth and Fifth Armies were concentrated in their respective areas ready for the imminent offensive – in which VI Corps at Anzio were to play a vital part – yet Kesselring was still unsure where the Allies planned to strike, and what role VI Corps intended to play.

There was, indeed, some doubt at VI Corps Headquarters itself precisely what form the Corps' contribution to the Allied offensive was to take. Truscott had devised four alternate plans and, having given each a code-name – Grasshopper, Crawdad, Turtle and Buffalo – he had discussed them in turn with Mark Clark. In addition to the plan for an attack on Valmontone south of the Alban Hills through Velletri – Operation Buffalo – there were plans for an attack in an easterly direction towards Sessi in support of the Fifth Army, and for breakouts towards Rome through Campoleone or, nearer to the coast, through Ardea.

On 5th May, General Alexander sailed across to the beachhead to discuss these plans in detail with Truscott. Truscott explained the plans, and the extent of his preparations with what he confessed was 'some measure of pride'. General Alexander 'let me know very quietly and firmly,' Truscott went on, 'that there was only one direction in which the attack should or would be launched, and that was from Cisterna to cut Highway 6 in the vicinity of Valmontone in the rear of the German main forces. He had, he said, reserved to himself the decision as to when he proposed to initiate it.'

After Alexander left Anzio that afternoon, General Truscott reported this conversation to Mark Clark. The next day Clark himself arrived at Anzio. He was evidently annoyed with what he took to be an attempt by the British to move in and run his Army and to interfere with the American

An attempt to sow discord by playing on inter-Allied resentment

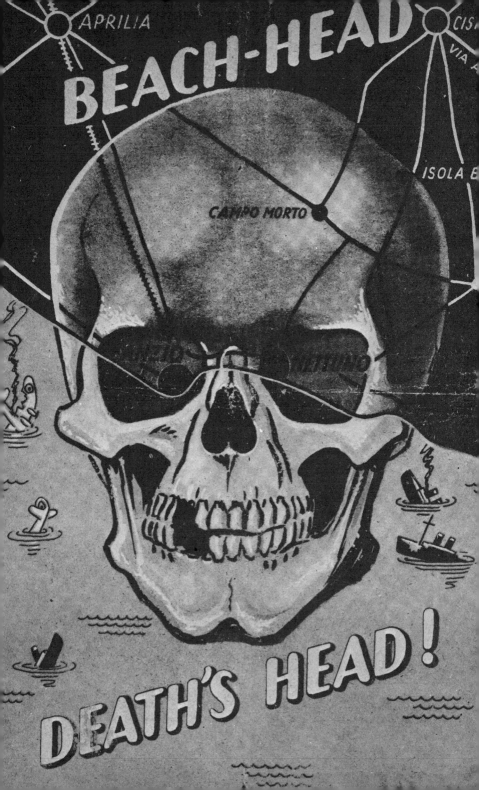

chain of command, and had already told Alexander this on the telephone. Clark was also sceptical, so he said later, that the Valmontone attack would result in the capture of the large number of prisoners which Alexander expected. It was 'far more likely', in his opinion, that the Germans' main forces would 'avoid capture by withdrawal northwards along a number of suitable axial roads that ran east of Rome. The trouble with [Operation Buffalo] was that, in order to get to Valmontone, the beachhead forces would more or less bypass the Alban Hills, leaving the enemy holding high ground that was vital to us if we were to enter Rome.'

And Clark had long since made up his mind that his Army should enjoy the glory of being first to enter and capture Rome. Admittedly the boundaries allotted by Alexander allowed for the Americans to achieve this ambition; but Clark was determined that nothing should interfere with its realisation. He told Truscott categorically that he himself would make the final decision as to the direction in which VI Corps should move once the German defences had been broken. Rather than provoke a serious collision with General Clark, Alexander did not insist that his orders should be obeyed.

Truscott, for his part, went on with his preparations for the mounting of Operation Buffalo in the middle of May. The main assault, through Cisterna and into the Velletri gap, between Alban Hills and the Colli Lepini, was to be made by the Americans. The capture of Cisterna was entrusted to the 3rd Division; the 1st Armoured Division was to advance to the west of the town, while the Special Service Force was to attack in the west towards Sezze so as to cut across Route 7. Once the area round Cisterna had been captured, the 36th Division was to pass through, and then, suppor-

The macabre Death's Head leaflet

ted by the 1st Armoured Division, it was to advance to the valley below Velletri. In the third stage of the attack the 36th Division and the 3rd Division were to advance together on Valmontone and Route 6. The American 45th Division was to be held in reserve after making a limited attack in the area of Carano. The British 1st and 5th Divisions were to make diversionary attacks across the Moletta in the west. The offensive was to be preceded by a succession of heavy air strikes – Operation Strangle – in which 26,000 tons of bombs were to be dropped on bridges, crossroads, viaducts, highways and factories behind the German lines. In their task of repelling the Allied breakout from Anzio, Kesselring and Mackensen had now lost the use of the Hermann Göring Division which had been ordered first towards Leghorn to deal with any possible Allied landing north of Rome and then to the southern front. Also, by 17th May, the 26th and 29th Panzer Grenadier Divisions had been transferred to the Tenth Army, so that the strength of German armour in the area had been considerably reduced. There was still, however, five divisions left to contain the Allies at Anzio, the 715th Division along the Mussolini Canal, the 362nd Division at Cisterna, the 3rd Panzer Grenadiers to their right, the 65th Division across the Albano-Anzio road and the 4th Parachute Division behind the Moletta.

Although they could not rely upon either the air support or, indeed, the artillery support that their opponents could command, Kesselring and Mackensen were satisfied that they would not easily be pushed back. Their troops had employed their time well in the past weeks, mining and wiring approaches, siting machine-gun nests and gun-emplacements, constructing weapons pits and dugouts. The Americans, who were to bear the burden of the Allied attack, would have to assault these strong defences uphill and across a network of drainage ditches and canals.

Breakout

'What we have always regarded as more important [than the capture of Rome] is the cutting off of as many German divisions as possible.' – Churchill to Stalin, 5th June 1944.

At eleven o'clock on the night of 11th May, on a sign broadcast by the BBC from London, the Allied artillery on

the southern front suddenly began the intensive barrage that heralded the opening of the great offensive. At midnight the Fifth and Eighth Armies moved forward to the attack.

Some three weeks earlier both the German Tenth Army's Commander-in-Chief, General von Vietinghoff, and the commander of the 14th Panzer Corps,

General von Senger und Etterlin, had been ordered back to the Führer's Headquarters to receive decorations and the customary exhortations that accompanied them. From there both of them had gone on leave. Von Senger's Chief of Staff was also on leave, and General Westphal, Kesselring's Chief of Staff, was ill. Thus four of the most important German officers in Italy were away from their various headquarters when they were most needed. By the time Vietinghoff and von Senger und Etterlin had hurried back the battle was well under way.

It was one of the most costly and hard-fought battles of the Italian campaign. The French Expeditionary Corps under Marshal Juin advanced to Monte Faito and reached the Liri north of Sant' Apollinaire; but the Polish Corps' brave attempts to advance up Monte Cairo and to surround Cassino monastery from the north failed with heavy losses; while the British XIII Corps had to fight hard to hold the bridgeheads it had secured across the Rapido; and the American II Corps, further to the west, found the going hard and slow. Gradually, however, German resistance began to weaken. XIII Corps pushed forward from its bridgeheads across the Rapido; the French Expeditionary Corps, in a brilliant attack, captured Monte Majo and Sant' Ambrogio, and, pressing forward up the Ausente Valley, took Ausonia. The Americans advanced to Santa Maria Infanta.

On 15th May, XIII Corps reached the Cassino-Pignatero road and the French entered San Giorgio; on the 16th the 78th Division reached Route 6. On the 17th after the Polish Corps had attacked again north of Cassino monastery and suffered further heavy casualties, Kesselring gave orders for the evacuation of the whole of the Cassino front, since the successes of

General Clark leads men of his VI Corps out of the beachhead to meet units of his II Corps coming north

Generals Vietinghoff and von Senger und Etterlin in retreat at last

the French and Americans in the south had rendered it untenable. That night the German 1st Paratroop Division began its retreat over the mountains to the west, and the next morning the Poles attacked the ruins of the monastery, now deserted except for the wounded whom the Germans had not been able to take away with them, and planted their red and white standard above them. By now, all along the front the Germans were in retreat; and the Hitler line which had been prepared behind the Gustav Line from Pontecorvo to Aquina and Piedimonte, was hurriedly re-named the Senger Line. Vietinghoff, back from leave, appealed to Kesselring for reinforcements to save his disintegrating front. The 71st Division was down to a hundred men; supplies and ammunition were almost exhausted; one battalion had been reduced to throwing rocks at the advancing army. But

Kesselring could do nothing to help him. If he reinforced Vietinghoff, how could Mackensen withstand the force of the Allies' imminent attack at Anzio?

The troops at Anzio anxiously awaited orders to break out of the beachhead. Many of them, hearing news and rumours from the south, had expected that their own attack would have begun long before this. A week had now passed, and still they had not moved. There was some opinion in London that, as Churchill told Alexander, 'it would have been better for the Anzio punch to have been let off first'.

Alexander replied to this on 18th May, pointing out that he had weighed very carefully the pros and cons of and Anzio breakout, and among many factors two had influenced him most. 'Firstly,' he wrote 'the enemy's reserves in that area were too strong and I wanted to draw them away first... Secondly, the Germans expected Anzio to be the major thrust, and to gain

surprise I did what he did not expect. I have ordered the 36th US Division to start moving into bridgehead tonight and I am trying to dribble them in unseen. When the right moment comes the Americans will punch out to get astride enemy's communications to Rome. If successful this may prove decisive.'

The time of the punch was fixed for 23rd May, to coincide with a fresh assault by the Eighth Army on the southern front. So as to be on hand to determine in person the direction that the punch would eventually take, General Clark left for Anzio to establish the advanced Headquarters of the Fifth Army in the Villa Borghese. For Clark, as he confessed, was 'shocked' that Alexander had made his plans for an attack in the direction of Valmontone without consulting him. 'I should point out at this time,' he wrote in his memoirs, 'that the Fifth Army had had an extremely difficult time through the whole campaign . . . We not only wanted the honour of capturing Rome,

but we felt we more than deserved it, that it would make up to a certain extent for the buffeting and the frustration we had undergone in keeping up the winter pressure against the Germans . . . Not only did we intend to become the first army in fifteen centuries to seize Rome from the south [he was forgetting Garibaldi], but we intended to see that the people at home knew that it was the Fifth Army that did the job, and knew the price that had been paid for it.'

Clark, in fact, was unashamedly determined that his Army alone must enjoy the triumph of capturing Rome and that, as he put it himself, no one else would 'get in on the act'. Alexander had assured him that this would be so, but he was not prepared to take his word for it.

The first attack was made an hour before dawn. It was the British diversionary attack across the mouth of the Moletta. It was a costly attack, strongly resisted, but it served its purpose. The Germans, under savage artillery bombardment since a quarter to six, believed for a time that the main attack was being made in this direction.

The real attack, made on Cisterna by the Americans, achieved the tactical surprise that Truscott had hoped for. But here, as on the southern front on 11th May, German resistance was fiercely determined. By the end of the day the 3rd Division was still fighting outside Cisterna; and the Second Combat Command of the 1st American Armoured Division, having suffered heavy casualties in the minefields that protected the German positions, had reached no further than the railroad embankment south of the town. The other Combat Command of the 1st Armoured, however, had used four of its 'snakes' to such good effect that it had blown wide paths through the minefields, enabling its leading units to rush across them at speed, throw the stunned Germans off the railroad tracks behind them and to advance almost half a mile beyond them. At the same time the men of the Special

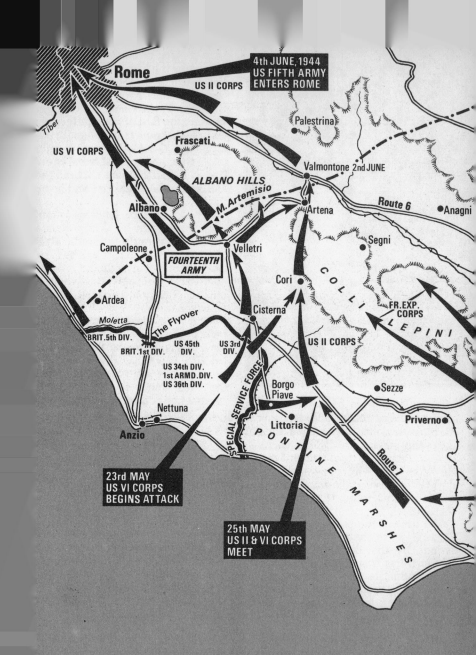

Rome

US II CORPS

**4th JUNE, 1944
US FIFTH ARMY
ENTERS ROME**

Tiber

US VI CORPS

Palestrina

Frascati

ALBANO HILLS

Valmontone 2nd JUNE

Albano

M. Artemisio

Artena

Route 6

Anagni

Campoleone

Velletri

**FOURTEENTH
ARMY**

Cori

Segni

COLLI

Ardea

Cisterna

FR. EXP.
CORPS

LEPINI

Moletta

The Flyover

BRIT.5th DIV.

BRIT.1st DIV.

US 45th
DIV.

US 3rd
DIV.

US II CORPS

US 34th DIV.
1st ARMD.DIV.
US 36th DIV.

SPECIAL SERVICE FORCE

Borgo
Piave

Sezze

Nettuna

Littoria

Priverno

Anzio

PONTINE

**23rd MAY
US VI CORPS
BEGINS ATTACK**

Route 7

MARSHES

**25th MAY
US II & VI CORPS
MEET**

T y r r h e n i a n

Attacks by 15th Army Group (Alexander)

German Defence Lines
- ——— Gustav Line
- — — — Hitler (Senger) Line
- —·—·— Ceasar Line

0   Miles   5   10   15
0   Kilometres   10   15   20

MONTI ERNICI

CAN.I CORPS

Sora

Frosinone

Arpino

BRIT.XIII CORPS

2300 HRS, 11th MAY ALLIED OFFENSIVE BEGINS

Sacco

Liri

1st PARA. DIV.

M. Caira

M. Cassino

POL.II CORPS

Rapido

Aquina

Cassino

TENTH ARMY

Liri

Pontecorvo

BRIT. EIGHTH ARMY

Pico

Pignataro

BRIT. XIII CORPS

MONTI AUSONI

San Giorgio

Sant' Apollin

Sant' Ambrogio

MONTI AURUNCI

Fondi

71st DIV.

M. Maio

Ausonia

M. Faito

FR. EXP. CORPS

US FIFTH ARMY

Terracina 22nd MAY

S. Maria Infante

Ausente

Garigliano

Sperlonga

Formia

US II CORPS

Gaeta

S e a

Even though the German troops were brilliantly led and fought with great determination, ultimately the Allies proved too strong for them and by late May and early June they were forced into a fighting withdrawal, leaving the way open for Clark's forces to enter Rome

Service Force, advancing to the east of Cisterna, fought their way to Route 7. In all, fifteen hundred German prisoners were captured that day. But the Americans had lost a hundred tanks and tank destroyers, and the 3rd Division alone had lost almost a thousand men.

The attack was resumed the next morning. Cisterna was by-passed by the 3rd Division which fought its way up towards the hill village of Cori; the 1st Armoured Division drove on towards Velletri; the 45th Division held off the German counterattacks on their left; while the British continued to press the enemy beyond the Moletta's mouth. Soon it was clear that the German defences were crumbling. The 715th Division had broken and was trying to withdraw towards the Lepini Hills; the 362nd Division

was struggling to hold on but was slowly losing its grasp of the northern shoulder of the breach that the Americans had driven into the German line. Units of the Hermann Göring Division, Kesselring's last reserve, were called in to dam the flood, moving by daylight so desperate was the situation, and suffering heavy casualties through air attacks, and the loss – so VI Corps claimed – of nearly a thousand vehicles destroyed or badly damaged.

By nightfall on 25th May, Cisterna had been cleared of its garrison, Cori had fallen, and the northern edges of the Colli Lepini were in American hands. It was now that Alexander expected Truscott to thrust on to Valmontone, to cut across Route 6. Indeed, on the morning of 26th May, Truscott – although VI Corps had by now suffered 2,872 casualties – was

sure that he could succeed in this objective, that he could force his way through the Velletri gap, and push past the reconnaissance units in Artena and Valontone. By so doing he would be able to check the retreat of the Germans now streaming north-wards from the broken southern front.

But that day he was prevented from carrying out this decision by a verbal order passed to him by the Fifth Army's operational staff. 'The Boss wants you to leave the 3rd Infantry Division and the Special Force to block Highway 6 and mount that assault you discussed with him to the northwest as soon as you can.'

Already, on the afternoon of 24th May, General Clark had asked Truscott if he had yet considered the possibility of halting the drive to Valmontone, and driving instead for the Alban Hills. Truscott had replied that he had thought about this, for a powerful and obvious move for the Velletri gap would give the Germans warning of his intentions and time for them to

escape the trap. But now there could be no escape, the collapse on the southern front had gone too far for that, and the resistance in the Velletri gap was not strong enough to prevent VI Corps reaching Valmontone and cutting off the Germans' retreat. And this, as Churchill persistently reminded Alexander, should now be the Allies' prime concern. 'It seems much more important to cut their line of retreat than anything else,' he wrote from London. 'A cop is much more impor-tant than Rome, which would anyhow come as its consequence. The cop is the only thing that matters.' Again, on the same day he wrote, 'I should feel myself wanting in comradeship if I did not let you know that the glory of this battle, already great, will be measured, not by the capture of Rome or the juncture with the bridgehead, but by the number of German divis-ions cut off. I am sure you will have resolved all this in your mind, and perhaps you have already acted in this way. Nevertheless I feel I ought to tell

149

you that it is the cop that counts.' Sharing Churchill's view, Truscott found it difficult to believe that Clark's eagerness to get to Rome had blinded him to the great opportunity now presented to the Allied armies. Before obeying the order to switch his attack to the Alban Hills, he tried to reach Clark by telephone, but Clark was not available. So the powerful drive to Valmontone was halted and the main part of the American forces turned left and made for the Alban Hills, Route 7 and Rome. It was not only his determination that his men should take Rome rather than the Eighth Army, which, in his opinion, had not made the most of their recent opportunities, that led Clark to make his decision. He did not believe that the British were advancing with sufficient force to trap the retreating Germans, and unless they did so there was no reason why he should direct VI Corps at Valmontone. But it was, undoubtedly, a Fifth Army capture of Rome that was uppermost in Clark's mind.

To comply in some degree with Alexander's orders, one Division, the 3rd, together with the 1st Special Service Force and part of the 1st Armoured Division, were kept on their original axis. They captured Artena without undue difficulty, but when they drove on to Valmontone, they were brought to a halt by units of the Hermann Göring Division, of the 362nd, 715th, 334th and of the 92nd Division, all of which were now established in the area holding open the withdrawal route. Unaided, the Americans were not strong enough to break the German hold on Route 6. So the retreating army escaped to the north, and Alexander's plan was thwarted. That, Churchill commented, was 'very unfortunate'. Clark's action, in Alexander's words, was 'inexplicable'.

For a time it seemed likely that General Clark's plan would be thwarted too. For the 34th, 36th, 45th and 1st Armoured Divisions, in their drive across the Alban Hills soon ran into stiff opposition along the Caesar Line,

a belt of strong points behind the Hitler (Senger) Line which had been built to cover Rome. Here the attack was halted, while skilful rearguard actions by the Germans extricated division after division of the Tenth Army, allowing them to get behind the Caesar Line alongside the Fourteenth Army. It appeared, indeed, that Kesselring might even be able to stabilise his line south of Rome and contain the Allied threat.

The impetus of VI Corps' attack was almost spent when General Clark regrouped the forces that were attacking the western end of the Caesar Line; and, no doubt, it would have ground to a halt altogether had not Mackensen failed to notice a gap in the Caesar Line at Velletri. When Kesselring detected it, he gave orders that it should be covered immediately. But before this could be done, the American 36th Division, commanded by Major-General Fred L Walker, had also discovered it.

The 36th, which faced the middle of

Below left: Breakout, and the Anzio troops reach Cisterna. *Above:* A haul of prisoners. *Below:* An Italian lends the weight of his expressive opinion to the German decline

the Alban Hills sector of the Caesar Line, between the 34th Division on its left and the 3rd Division on its right, had sent out numerous patrols on the night of 30th May, hoping to find a way of out flanking the German positions at Velletri. One of these patrols found Monte Artemisio, the commanding height behind the town, unoccupied. Two regiments came up onto it, while a third cut through behind Velletri to prevent the garrison's retreat.

With this gap in the Caesar Line opened up in front of him General Clark saw and seized his opportunity. He ordered II Corps to renew its attack on Valmontone and to cut across Route 6, VI Corps to drive round the southwestern side of the hills, and the

Left : The Fifth Army enters Rome.
Below : The people pack St Peter's Square for Pope Pius XII's blessing

36th Division to push through the centre, exploiting the gap it had found. Simultaneously, the two British Divisions, the 1st and 5th, were to advance along the coast.

The battle that ensued was again a fierce one, but by 2nd June when II Corps captured Valmontone its issue was no longer in doubt. That night the Hermann Göring and 344th Divisions withdrew east of Rome, opening up the way to Route 6. The remaining units of the Fourteenth Army then had also been compelled to retire. They pulled across the Tiber east of Rome.

Kesselring offered to make Rome an open city, but the Allies considered the undertaking to carry out no troop movements in the capital both 'belated and insincere'. Nevertheless, when the leading American units entered Rome on 4th June, they found all the bridges intact.

Clark gets his dream

The men of the 88th Division entered Piazza Venezia at a quarter to seven in the evening to the cheers of excited crowds. King Victor Emmanual abdicated and installed his son as Regent; Field-Marshal Badoglio resigned as Prime Minister and his place was taken by the elderly anti-Fascist Ivanhoe Bonomi, who had been ousted from the Socialist Party by Mussolini in 1912.

While Mark Clark enjoyed his deserved triumph, the Eighth Army continued its advance towards Terni; for Alexander was anxious to push Kesselring as far as the northern Appenines before he had time to reorganise his forces.

'What we have always regarded as more important [than the capture of Rome],' Churchill added in a letter to Stalin on 5th June when conveying to him the good news of the fall of the first Axis capital, 'is the cutting off of as many enemy divisions as possible. General Alexander is now ordering strong armoured forces northward on Terni, which should largely complete the cutting off of all the divisions which were sent by Hitler to fight south of Rome.'

But Alexander was seriously hampered by the lack of open ground in which he could use his tanks. He had two fresh armoured divisions in hand, yet he could not make use of them effectively. 'If only the country were more open,' he commented in a signal, 'we would make hay of the whole lot.'

As it was, the German Army, while severely battered, was still a coherent force. Kesselring was able to take it north across the Arno and to make a new stand behind the Gothic Line; and although he had suffered heavy losses, including 18,000 prisoners, the Allies had suffered badly, too. The Eighth Army had lost 6,000 men; the Fifth Army no less than 35,000 men of whom 3,500 were British, 10,500 were French and the great majority – 21,000 – American.

Post-Mortem

On 5th June, 1944, Stalin sent a message to Churchill: 'I congratulate you on the great victory of the Allied Anglo-American forces – the taking of Rome. This news has been greeted in the Soviet Union with great satisfaction.'

It was, indeed, a great victory, but ever since its achievement two questions have constantly been asked: could it not have been much greater, and who was to blame that it was not?

Churchill himself decided, after the war was over, that the 'aggressive action of our armies in Italy, and specifically the Anzio stroke, made its full contribution towards the success of "Overlord".' German divisions had been drawn into Italy and several of them had been destroyed. The amphibious operation 'did not immediately fructify', he had to admit, but he assured Stalin, it was a 'correct strategic move and brought its reward in the end'.

In a letter to Field-Marshal Smuts, written at the end of February 1944 when the savage fighting at Anzio had ended in stalemate, Churchill took credit for getting 'this big amphibious operation soundly organised'; but he went on to explain that his efforts did not extend to the conduct of the battle, 'which of course I left altogether to the commanders'. And it was these commanders whom he blamed for the 'frittering away of a brilliant opening in which fortune and design had played their part'. He did not blame Alexander in whom his confidence remained undiminished; he did not blame Truscott whom everyone spoke of 'most highly'. But he did blame both Clark and Lucas. 'In all his talk with me,' Churchill continued his letter to Smuts, 'Alexander envisaged that the essence of the battle was the seizure of the Alban Hills with the utmost speed, and to this end I was able to obtain from the United States their 504th Parachute Regiment, although at the time it was under orders to return for "Overlord". But at the last moment General Clark cancelled the use of this regiment, and the American General Lucas, a man of fifty-five who at Salerno had distinguished himself in command of a corps, seems to have had the idea in his mind that at all costs he must be prepared for a counterattack. As a result, although directly I learned the landing was successful I sent Alexander injunctions that he should dig

out claims rather than consolidate bridgeheads, the whole operation became stagnant.'

Alexander, in subsequently published statements, agreed with Churchill that the plan failed through lack of boldness in the early stages. 'The commander of the assault Corps, the American General Lucas, missed his opportunities by being too slow and cautious,' Alexander decided. 'He failed to realise the great advantages that surprise had given him. He allowed Time to beat him.' In his memoirs, Alexander repeated this criticism, substituting the word 'surprise' for 'Time', and going on to say that Lucas was too concerned with the worry that he would have to fight his way ashore as his men had had to do at Salerno. 'On finding that he was not opposed he was taken by surprise and unable to adjust his mind to a new situation. A younger or more experienced soldier would have been quicker to react.' Nevertheless, Alexander felt compelled to admit that the Alban Hills were 'really a massive mountain terrain, much more difficult to gain and maintain than can be apparent from maps. And to have secured the hills and kept open the line of com-

munications to Anzio would not have been an easy task... It is interesting to consider what our position would have been if the fresh German divisions had found us stretched from Anzio to the Alban Hills. Could we have maintained our beachhead intact on such a wide perimeter with the troops at our disposal? We had no more than two divisions and it would have been disastrous for our ultimate operation if Anzio had been wiped out'.

In Field-Marshal Kesselring's opinion, the 'basic error' was this weakness of the striking forces to which Alexander drew attention, a weakness dictated by the number of landing craft available, and by the number of troops in the area that could be spared either from the Cassino front or elsewhere. As an offensive it was no more than 'a half-way measure'; and with but two divisions at their disposal, 'it would have been the Anglo-American doom to over-extend themselves. The landing force was initially too weak'.

Certainly, even though no early effort was made to reach the Alban Hills, the Allies could not possibly have held their ground at Anzio, had it not been for the dogged determination of the American and British soldiers and the support they received from the naval forces. But if Lucas was, perhaps, right not to risk his Corps by striking out for the Alban Hills and Rome, might he not have been well advised to seize the nearer and, as it was soon to prove, vital positions of Campoleone and Cisterna? These both could have been taken without undue risk within the first twenty-four hours.

Yet Lucas's caution was not entirely his own fault. There stood behind him the dominating figure of his Army commander, General Clark; and there was always in his mind Clark's urgent advice given just before the convoys were due to sail out of the Bay of Naples: 'Don't stick your neck out as I did at Salerno'.

Both Clark and Lucas were painfully aware that the Italian campaign and, in particular, the Anzio operation, were peculiarly British concerns. Lucas was always conscious of the feeling that he and his American soldiers were being pushed into a venture in which he, for one, could discern 'no military reason'. It threatened another Gallipoli and 'apparently the same amateur' – Churchill, the British Prime Minister – was 'still on the coach's bench'. If all went well with Churchill's gamble, Churchill would receive the credit, if the gamble failed, Lucas and Clark were the players who would lose all.

Mark Clark was even more conscious of this than John Lucas was. He strongly resented the fact that since Eisenhower's departure he had had to submit to British control; and he did not have any high opinion of British methods: the British were too slow, too easy-going, too satisfied with their traditions. He had unwillingly to accept Alexander as his superior, but he was determined to reserve the right to lead his own American army as he thought right. And, indeed, it has to be said that Alexander allowed him to do so where a sterner, more ruthless commander would have insisted upon his orders being obeyed.

Clark, of course, was not an easy man for an English general to handle.

He was extremely charming and extremely talented, he fully deserved the reputation he had acquired and was to enhance. But his concern for publicity seemed to the British wholly misplaced in a fighting soldier. Montgomery's – and, indeed, Patton's – self-advertisement would have been quite intolerable without their brilliant military successes to justify them; yet Montgomery's and Patton's military successes were there for all to admire. Although he had demonstrated his worth at Salerno, Mark Clark had not yet won a comparable reputation, and he was determined to do so.

It must be immediately said that his determination arose from as deep a concern for his soldiers' reputation as for his own. He was convinced that his army had earned the right to reap the rewards of the Italian campaign by their achievements, sufferings and exertions. It was they who had endured the battle of Salerno, while Montgomery's Eighth Army had come across little opposition in their advance from Reggio – and a slow advance it had been; yet the accounts of the British progress which had emanated from Alexander's headquarters to the outside world had made it seem that the British rather than the Americans were the heroes of the hour. This, Clark was resolved, would not happen again.

If faults can be found with the commanders, however, there are deeper reasons for the failure of the Anzio venture to fulfil the hopes that had been entertained for it.

Operation Shingle was not only prepared in too great a hurry and with too few troops, it disastrously divided the Allies' strength in Italy. Cassino is well over sixty miles from Anzio as the crow flies, far too far for either front to support the other. On neither front were the Allies powerful enough to break through the German defences until reinforcements arrived from North Africa, the Middle-East and, above all, America.

Discussions about the validity of Operation Shingle are, of course, inseparable from the more important question: was the Italian campaign as a whole justified at all? Did it succeed in keeping tied down in the peninsula sufficient German forces, in relation to the Allied strength employed, fundamentally to affect the ultimate outcome of the war?

In October 1943 eighteen German divisions had been drawn into Italy to meet the Allied invasion force of fifteen divisions; a further fifteen German divisions were, at that time, stationed in the Balkans as a result of the Italian surrender. In all, therefore, thirty-three German divisions were held in southern Europe.

If the Americans had had their way, the Allies would have remained content with this. Two important objects had been achieved: one of the Axis partners had been forced out of the war, and valuable airfields in southern Italy were in Allied hands. But the British view that the Germans should be driven northwards in Italy prevailed; and the cost to the Allied effort was a heavy one.

The Allies were obliged to increase their strength in Italy in the spring of 1944 to twenty-three divisions, while the Germans – largely due to the great advantages which the geography of Italy bestows upon its defenders – were able to contain them with twenty-two. And few of these twenty-two German divisions were more than two-thirds the strength of their opponents'. By June 1944, when Operation Overlord was launched, Allied strength in Italy had increased yet again to thirty divisions, whereas the Germans were still able to hold them with twenty-two. By outnumbering the enemy's front line troops by four to one, the Allies were at last able to break through the Gustav Line. But they were still unable to destroy Kesselring's army which reorganised itself north of the Arno. As Sir Basil Liddell Hart has observed, 'the continuation of the Allied offensive in Italy had not proved a good strategic investment'.

Yet, although this verdict cannot seriously be questioned, and although the Anzio operation cannot be judged otherwise than as a gamble that failed, its failure was not complete.

Had it failed utterly, had the Allies been driven into the sea, the Germans would have been given an invaluable, if temporary, respite; they would have been enabled to reduce the strength of their forces in Italy and to build up their defences in northern Europe.

Hitler recognised this. He believed that the Allies, rather than batter their way up the Italian peninsula, would rely on their control of the sea to make a series of amphibious attacks not only in the Mediterranean, but also in the Aegean, on the western coast of France, even perhaps in the Iberian peninsula, as preludes to their main assault in northwestern France. As the first of these preliminary amphibious assaults, the landing at Anzio must be checked and the Allies thrown off the beaches. He foresaw, as he told his commanders and his soldiers, that from a German victory at Anzio great political as well as great military advantages would follow. Indeed, had he dared to weaken other exposed parts of his European fortress these advantages would almost certainly have followed. But they did not follow. Hitler failed to win the victory he so badly needed at Anzio, just as the Allies failed to break the Italian stalemate by landing there.

For the Allies, though, the gamble at Anzio did not represent a total loss. Valuable lessons were learned and were remembered. Operation Shingle had signally failed, as Alexander had confidently assured Lucas, to make Operation Overlord unnecessary. But by so clearly exposing the dangers of not making the initial landings in sufficient strength and of not pressing forward immediately to important points inland, Shingle made an undoubted contribution to Overlord's ultimate success.

Bibliography

Anzio Winford Vaughan-Thomas (Pan Books, London. Holt, Rinehart and Winston, New York)

Anzio: the gamble that failed Martin Blumenson (Weidenfeld and Nicholson, London. Lippencott, Philadelphia)

The Battle for Italy W G F Jackson (Batsford, London. Harper and Row, New York)

The Italian Campaign 1943–45: a political and military re-assessment G A Shepperd (Barker, London. Praeger, New York)

Closing the Ring: The Second World War volume V Sir Winston Churchill (Cassell, London. Houghton Mifflin, Boston)

A Don at War David Hunt (Kimber, London)

The Fortress Raleigh Trevelyan (Collins, London)

Calculated Risk M W Clark (Harrap, London. Harper and Row, New York)

Triumph of the West Sir Arthur Bryant (Collins, London. Doubleday, New York)

Command Decision edited by Kent Roberts Greenfield (Methuen, London. Harcourt, New York)

The Memoirs of Field-Marshal Kesselring (Kimber, London. Athenäum Verlag, Frankfurt)

Command Mission Lucian K Truscott (Dutton, New York)

History of the Second World War volume V John Ehrman (HMSO, London)

Report by the Supreme Allied Commander Mediterranean to the Chief of Staff (HMSO, London)

The German Army in the West Siegfried Westphal (Cassell, London. Athenäum Verlag, Frankfurt)

The Alexander Memoirs (Cassell, London)